JOURNEYS

Benchmark and Unit Tests

Grade 4

HOUGHTON MIFFLIN HARCOURT
School Publishers

"Sandy Skyscrapers to Clay Cobras" by Julie Brooks Hiller, P.G., illustrated by Karen Dugan from *Spider* magazine, April 2006. Text copyright © 2006 by Carus Publishing Company. Illustrations copyright © 2006 by Karen Dugan. Reprinted by permission of The Cricket Magazine Group, a division of Carus Publishing Company.

"Digging for Africa's Lost Dinosaurs" by Lesley Reed from *Appleseeds* magazine, January 2005. Text copyright © 2005 by Carus Publishing Company. Reprinted by permission of Cobblestone Publishing, Inc, a division of Carus Publishing Company.

"A Tree Needs a Special Place" by Lyda Williamson, illustrated by Laura Jacobsen from *Highlights for Children* magazine, April 2005. Copyright © 2005 by Highlights for Children, Inc. Reprinted by permission of Highlights for Children, Inc.

"The Library" from *Once Inside the Library* by Barbara Huff. Text copyright © 1957, renewed 1985 by Barbara A. Huff. Reprinted by permission of Little, Brown & Company, Inc.

"Fly High, Bessie Coleman" by Jane Sutcliffe in *Highlights for Children* magazine, February 2004. Text copyright © 2004 by Highlights for Children, Inc. Reprinted by permission of Highlights for Children, Inc.

Copyright © by Houghton Mifflin Harcourt Publishing Company

All rights reserved. No part of this work may be reproduced or transmitted in any form or by any means, electronic or mechanical, including photocopying or recording, or by any information storage or retrieval system, without the prior written permission of the copyright owner unless such copying is expressly permitted by federal copyright law.

Permission is hereby granted to individuals using the corresponding student's textbook or kit as the major vehicle for regular classroom instruction to photocopy copying masters from this publication in classroom quantities for instructional use and not for resale. Requests for information on other matters regarding duplication of this work should be addressed to Houghton Mifflin Harcourt Publishing Company, Attn: Contracts, Copyrights, and Licensing, 9400 South Park Center Loop, Orlando, Florida 32819.

Printed in the U.S.A.

ISBN-13: 978-0-54-736888-7
ISBN-10: 0-54-736888-7

9 10 0982 18 17 16 15 14 13 12 11
4500325989

If you have received these materials as examination copies free of charge, Houghton Mifflin Harcourt Publishing Company retains title to the materials and they may not be resold. Resale of examination copies is strictly prohibited.

Possession of this publication in print format does not entitle users to convert this publication, or any portion of it, into electronic format.

Contents

© Houghton Mifflin Harcourt Publishing Company. All rights reserved.

Name _____ Date _____

Reading

> **Read this selection. Then answer the questions that follow it.**
> **Mark your answers on the Answer Document.**

An Art Project

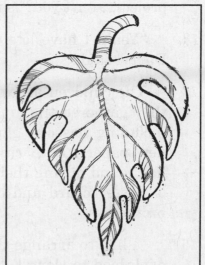

1   As Kasara and her brother, Darryl, strolled to school, Kasara stopped to pick up a feather, and a few minutes later, a leaf from an oak tree.

2   "What are you doing, Kasara?" Darryl inquired.

3   "I'm collecting objects to create a collage," Kasara explained.

4   "What's a collage?" Darryl asked.

5   "Collage is a kind of art in which you arrange a lot of different kinds of objects and scraps on a piece of paper or cardboard, and then you glue them in place," Kasara explained. "What you get is a unique collection of colors and textures. My class has made collages a couple of times already this year."

6   "Other than feathers and leaves and scraps, what kinds of objects do you use?" Darryl asked.

7   "You can use just about anything you want. Caps of soda bottles, plastic packaging, old postage stamps, and greeting cards are some things I've used, and this time, I'm also going to cut words and pictures out of old magazines and newspapers. You can even draw or paint on a collage if you want," said Kasara.

8   "That sounds like fun. Can I make a collage too?" Darryl asked.

9   "Sure. We can work on it together after we finish our homework tonight," answered Kasara.

GO ON ▶

© Houghton Mifflin Harcourt Publishing Company. All rights reserved.

Name _____ Date _____

10   During the rest of the walk to school, Darryl looked for objects he could use to create his collage, and he continued to look for more things as he walked home that afternoon.

11   He found a piece of string, some shiny, colorful paper, and even some bark from a tree.

12   Kasara laughed as she watched him. "You're excited about this project, aren't you?" she asked.

13   "Yeah! I have lots of ideas about how I want my collage to look," Darryl said.

14   The children arrived at home and first did their homework. Then they gathered the art supplies they would need to make the collage, including scissors, glue, markers, and a stack of old magazines and newspapers. Both children placed on the table all the objects they had found during their walk, and then Kasara unrolled a large piece of poster board and cut it in half; half for herself and half for her brother.

15   "I like to arrange the objects before I glue anything down," Kasara explained to Darryl. "That way, I can make changes if I want to, but once the objects are glued on, the collage is pretty <u>permanent</u>."

16   The children worked together for the rest of the evening. After a few hours, they had glued everything in place and set the collages aside for the glue to dry thoroughly. The next morning, they each went to check on their completed projects.

17   Darryl looked at his sister and grinned. "You're the official art instructor of the family now. What will tomorrow's art project be?" he asked. She laughed and ruffled his hair.

© Houghton Mifflin Harcourt Publishing Company. All rights reserved.

1 Kasara thought Darryl was excited about making a collage because he—

   A started his collage the minute he finished his homework

   B told Kasara that he had lots of ideas about making a collage

   C started looking everywhere for objects for his collage

   D asked Kasara if he could make a collage when she made hers

2 What does the word <u>permanent</u> mean in paragraph 15?

   F Flexible

   G Unchangeable

   H Interesting

   J Perfect

3 As Darryl worked on his collage, he probably—

   A told Kasara a better way to arrange her objects on the poster board

   B arranged his objects before he glued any of them down

   C made a few changes to his collage after he had glued down the objects

   D removed objects after he had arranged all the objects

4 According to the story, Darryl thinks his sister—

   F is a good teacher

   G likes to learn from others

   H most enjoys working alone

   J likes to try new things more than he does

5 Which most likely happened in the days after the story ended?

   A Kasara will teach Darryl how to do other kinds of art.

   B Darryl will tell Kasara he does not enjoy making art.

   C The collages Kasara and Darryl made will fall apart.

   D Kasara will decide she would rather work by herself.

GO ON

© Houghton Mifflin Harcourt Publishing Company. All rights reserved.

> **Read this selection. Then answer the questions that follow it.**
> **Mark your answers on the Answer Document.**

Uninvited Guests

1   Our country has been invaded! However, it's not people who are the invaders. It's plants and animals.

2   These plants and animals are native to other parts of the world and were brought to North America. When transplanted out of their native environment, they can damage their new homes. They cause disease, wipe out native plants and animals, and cost a lot of money to control or eliminate.

3   What are some of the plants and animals that are causing trouble, and how did they get here? One such plant is called kudzu, a vine that was brought to the United States from Japan in 1876.

4   At first, kudzu was a well-liked plant, admired for the color of its flowers. It also appeared to be useful because it could keep soil from washing away. However, the vine grows very fast; too fast. Kudzu covers land that people need for forestry and farming. It can kill trees and shrubs by uprooting them or blocking out sunlight.

5   Similarly, a problematic animal, native to Central and South America, is the giant toad. The giant toad grows to be six inches long. (That's long for a toad.) The people who brought this toad to the United States wanted it to eat certain bugs that were eating crops. Unfortunately, the toads have many babies. These toads are also very poisonous. Other animals that eat the toads can become sick or may even die.

© Houghton Mifflin Harcourt Publishing Company. All rights reserved.

6   A non-native insect that is very troublesome is the fire ant. Not only can it damage crops, it also protects other insects that hurt the crops. Fire ants have actually destroyed roads by removing the dirt from under the road bed.

7   When fire ants are disturbed, they swarm and bite. The ant bites hurt, itch, and burn. If the ants are swarming, it is possible for a person to be stung hundreds of times.

8   Plants and animals that are not native to this environment can be pests. It can cost a lot of money to get rid of them. They can destroy crops and forests. They can also harm the plants and animals that are native to an area. It is better to think carefully before transplanting a plant or animal from its native environment to a new one.

© Houghton Mifflin Harcourt Publishing Company. All rights reserved.

6 Which words from the article have almost the same meaning?

   F *live in, invade*

   G *troublesome, harmful*

   H *native, new*

   J *wipe out, eliminate*

7 What is the main reason the author believes that kudzu is a pest?

   A It takes over land and plants.

   B It is not useful to people.

   C It costs a lot of money to control.

   D It makes animals sick when they eat it.

8 Kudzu and the giant toad are alike because both—

   F are known to cause diseases

   G can make people itch or burn

   H can make animals sick if they are eaten

   J were brought to the United States to be helpful

9 What does the word <u>transplanting</u> mean in paragraph 8?

   A Planting different things at different times

   B Planting the same thing more than one time

   C Moving something from one place to another

   D Being able to be moved from one place to another

10 This article is mainly about plants and animals that—

   F damage crops

   G come from other places and do harm

   H have become popular in the United States

   J cause people to feel sick

© Houghton Mifflin Harcourt Publishing Company. All rights reserved.

> **Read this selection. Then answer the questions that follow it.**
> **Mark your answers on the Answer Document.**

Sanjay's Rakhi

1   Nina and her mother perused the marketplace, examining rows and rows of tables groaning with the weight of homemade food, jewelry, and paper cut-outs. Stopping at one table, Nina's mother held up a bracelet made of thread. "What about this rakhi for Sanjay?" she said.

2   Nina looked at the rakhi in her mother's hand. "It's nice," she said. "But this Raksha Bandhan, I want Sanjay's rakhi to be special. I'm going to keep looking." Nina turned back to the display of rakhis.

3   Tomorrow was Raksha Bandhan. This festival was always held on a full moon in August. Raksha Bandhan was a holiday just for siblings. On this day, brothers and sisters declared their affection and devotion for each other with words, rituals, and small gifts. Sisters wished their brothers well. Brothers promised to protect sisters from harm.

4   Nina had always loved celebrating Raksha Bandhan with her brother Sanjay. Each year they would look forward to the holiday, the special dishes, and the presents. But this year the festival meant more to her than it had in the past.

5   Sanjay was walking home from school one day that spring when he saw Nina surrounded by a group of older students. At first he was glad that she had made some new friends. But when he approached them, he saw that one of the boys held Nina's schoolbooks. Papers and pencils were scattered on the ground, and Nina was crouching on the ground, crying.

6   Sanjay pushed the boys aside and knelt down beside Nina. "Come on, let's go home," he said gently. He helped her gather her things, and with a scathing glance at the bullies, he led her away. No one from school had teased his little sister since then.

7   Raksha Bandhan was a time for honoring the bond between brothers and sisters, but until now, Nina had treated it like any other fun holiday. Since Sanjay had stood up for her, she understood what it meant to him to promise his protection. The festival now held more significance for Nina than ever. She had decided to buy Sanjay the most beautiful rakhi she could afford.

8   Nina wandered over to another table and looked at the rakhis. Right away one caught her eye. This rakhi had a band made of brightly colored thread. In the center was a sunburst of gold paper and turquoise beads. She grinned when the salesman told her how much the rakhi cost.

9   "Mom, I found it!" Nina cried. "Look what I'm going to give Sanjay!"

GO ON

11 In the story, Nina decides—

A why she wants to buy a special rakhi

B which rakhi to buy for her brother

C what gifts she will receive at the festival

D what dishes she will cook for the festival

12 Most of the story takes place at—

F Nina and Sanjay's house

G the market

H the festival

J Nina and Sanjay's school

13 Which of the following will most likely happen next?

A Nina will buy the rakhi for Sanjay.

B Nina will continue to shop for rakhis.

C Nina will ask her mother to buy the rakhi.

D Nina will promise to protect Sanjay.

14 Which word best describes Nina in this story?

F Upset

G Thankful

H Unsure

J Helpful

15 Which sentence best describes the theme of the story?

A A gift is only good if it costs a lot of money.

B Preparing for a festival takes a lot of time.

C Sometimes people need help in picking the perfect gift.

D Giving gifts is as rewarding as receiving them.

> **Read this selection. Then answer the questions that follow it.**
> **Mark your answers on the Answer Document.**

Sandy Skyscrapers to Clay Cobras

by Julie Brooks Hiller, P.G.
art by Karen Dugan

1   What in the world is coating your sneakers? Is *silt* stuck between the zigzags? Is *clay* caked to your laces? Is *sand* scraping your toes? *Gravel* gouging your heel? A soil scientist knows the difference between silt, clay, sand, and gravel. Do you?

2   It's simple, if you remember it's only a matter of size.

3   Sand and gravel are made of different-sized pieces of rock. Gravel is made up of coarser rock about the size of a marble or larger. Sand is tiny, fine, and gritty, about the size of a freckle—perfect for building sandy skyscrapers at the shore!

4   Silt and clay are also made of rock, but the pieces are so tiny that you can't see them with the naked eye. So how can you tell the difference without a microscope? Your fingers can figure it out. Soil with lots of silt in it feels creamy, like buttery icing. Soil with lots of clay in it feels sticky and rolls between your fingers like modeling clay— perfect for creating clay cobras!

5   Most folks have a mixture of gravel, sand, clay, and silt in their backyards. What's in yours? If you live on a beach, you may have only one type of soil—sand. If you live inland, perhaps you'll find all four types. Wherever you live, if you enjoy getting messy, you'll have fun performing this experiment to find out. It's as easy as pie—*mud* pie.

GO ON

© Houghton Mifflin Harcourt Publishing Company. All rights reserved.

Name _____   Date _____

What You'll Need:

> 1-quart bucket or bowl
> hand shovel
> 1 cup water
> finely meshed wire sieve
> 1 gallon water for washing
> playclothes

What to Do:

1. Use the hand shovel to dig a soil sample from the yard. (Ask an adult where you may dig.)

2. Fill the bucket or bowl half full with soil.

3. Add 1/2 cup water and mix with your hands until the thick mud sticks together like a giant meatball. Add more water if the soil is still too dry. Be careful not to add too much water. It will make the soil soupy.

4. Rub your fingers together and feel the soil texture. Do you feel rock pieces about as big as marbles? If so, you have gravel in your soil. Does it feel gritty, like sandpaper? If so, you have sand in your soil. Does it coat your skin and feel creamy, like buttery icing? If so, you have silt in your soil. Does it feel sticky, and can you roll it into a snake shape? If so, you have clay in your soil.

5. To better see the sand and gravel, put the soil into the sieve and rinse the silt and clay away with water until only rock pieces are left. What colors do you see? Are the pieces rounded or angular?

6. Congratulations! You've just completed tests done by real soil scientists, and you've discovered what kinds of soil are in your own backyard! (Don't forget to wash up before going into your house!)

GO ON

© Houghton Mifflin Harcourt Publishing Company. All rights reserved.

16 Sand, gravel, silt, and clay all are alike because they—

F are all made of rock

G are all bigger than a freckle

H can all be found at or near a beach

J can all be seen without a microscope

17 In which step do you test the soil by feeling it?

A 1

B 3

C 4

D 6

18 According to the article, how would the reader know if there was gravel in the soil?

F It would contain rock pieces.

G It would feel like sand paper.

H It would coat your skin.

J It would feel sticky.

19 Which sentence from the article states a fact?

A *Soil with lots of clay in it feels sticky and rolls between your fingers like modeling clay—perfect for creating clay cobras!*

B *A soil scientist knows the difference between silt, clay, sand, and gravel.*

C *Wherever you live, if you enjoy getting messy, you'll have fun performing this experiment to find out.*

D *Sand is tiny, fine, and gritty, about the size of a freckle—perfect for building sandy skyscrapers at the shore!*

20 Which part of the directions is most important to follow?

F Mixing the right amount of water in with the soil

G Making sure the skin is fully coated with soil

H Making sure the snake shape is long

J Using the right kind of bucket

GO ON

© Houghton Mifflin Harcourt Publishing Company. All rights reserved.

> **Read this selection. Then answer the questions that follow it.**
> **Mark your answers on the Answer Document.**

Jeff's Journal

September 2

1   When I grow up I want to be a chef. My friends think I am crazy; they say cooking is for girls. I don't care what they say. I watch cooking shows on television, and many of the stars on those shows are men.

2   I've already learned a lot about what it takes to be a chef. The library had some books about cooking. One book said that, in French, the word "chef" means boss or chief in French. One day, I will be the boss of a kitchen.

3   Another book explained all about the different jobs for the people who prepare food. A restaurant kitchen is a busy place! Prep cooks clean the food, slice fruits and vegetables, and chop other ingredients. Pastry specialists prepare dough for baked goods and arrange fancy desserts just before they are served. Cooks on the "hot line" prepare fish and meat entrees that are served hot to waiting customers.

4   Apparently becoming a lead chef is not easy. You must go to school and practice for years. In college I plan to study the culinary arts and learn about becoming a chef. They teach you how to prepare food, cook different <u>dishes</u>, and how to make food appear attractive when it is served. When I finish college, I would like to study more in another country. Right now, my first choice is Italy, but I might change my mind when I get older.

5   Both my mom and dad love to cook, and they let me help them shop, plan meals, and even do some of the cooking. Maybe that's why my goal is to be a chef when I grow up.

© Houghton Mifflin Harcourt Publishing Company. All rights reserved.

21 According to Jeff's journal entry, before slicing fruits and vegetables, prep cooks need to—

A serve the waiting customers

B chop the ingredients

C arrange the desserts

D clean the food

22 The main job of a cook on the "hot line" is—

F to prepare meat and fish dishes

G to make the food look nice before it is served

H to prepare fancy desserts

J to bake pastries

23 In paragraph 4, the word <u>dishes</u> means—

A gives out

B gossips

C plates

D meals

24 Which of the following best describes why Jeff might want to study cooking in another country?

F To learn more about the cooking in that country

G To move farther away from his parents

H To enjoy himself after college

J To become a lead chef

25 What is the main reason Jeff learned to love to cook?

A Looking forward to being a boss

B Watching shows on television

C Cooking with his parents

D Reading about cooking

26 Based on his journal entry, which word best describes Jeff?

F Dedicated

G Unsure

H Bossy

J Funny

GO ON

© Houghton Mifflin Harcourt Publishing Company. All rights reserved.

Name _____ Date _____

> **Read this selection. Then read answer the questions that follow it.**
> **Mark your answer on the Answer Document.**

The American Flag

An Early American Flag

1   Before the end of the war for independence from Britain, Americans had many different flags. Then the first unofficial American flag appeared. This American flag had the British flag in the upper left-hand corner. The rest of the flag was covered with red and white stripes.

The First Official Flag

2   When America won its freedom, Americans wanted a new flag. They did not want a flag that looked like Britain's. American leaders met to talk about what the new flag should look like.

3   On June 14, 1777, Congress passed the first flag resolution. It said that the American flag would have 13 red and white stripes and that there would be 13 white stars against a blue background.

4   No one knows for sure who came up with the idea for how the first American flag should look. Francis Hopkinson, who helped develop government <u>seals</u>, may have helped. Credit sometimes also goes to Betsy Ross, who some believe sewed the first American flag.

5   After the war, each star and each stripe represented the 13 colonies. It was decided that the number of stars would change each time a new state joined the union, but the number of stripes would stay the same.

Flag Code Rules

6   In 1923, leaders met in Washington D.C. to create a set of rules for how to handle the American flag. In 1942, these rules became official. They are known as the Flag Code.

© Houghton Mifflin Harcourt Publishing Company. All rights reserved.

Name _____ Date _____

7   Here are a few of the rules:

  • The flag should be raised quickly, but lowered slowly.

  • The flag should not be flown in bad weather, unless it is an all-weather flag.

  • The flag should never touch the ground.

  • The flag should be flown at night only if it is well lighted.

Today's Flag

8   The flag we have now dates from July 4, 1960, when Hawaii became a state. That increased the number of stars on the flag to 50. Our American flag has a rich history. We can be proud of the Stars and Stripes.

9   Read about other important events related to the flag throughout history.

Flag Events in History

1777	Continental Congress adopts the following: *Resolved: that the flag of the United States be thirteen stripes, alternate red and white; that the union be thirteen stars, white in a blue field, representing a new constellation.* (The stars represent Delaware, Pennsylvania, New Jersey, Georgia, Connecticut, Massachusetts, Maryland, South Carolina, New Hampshire, Virginia, New York, North Carolina, and Rhode Island.)
1814	Francis Scott Key writes "The Star-Spangled Banner." It officially becomes the national anthem in 1931.
1869	The first flag appears on a postage stamp.
1960	The 50th star is added to the flag as Hawaii becomes a state.
1969	The American flag is placed on the moon by Neil Armstrong.

© Houghton Mifflin Harcourt Publishing Company. All rights reserved.

Name _____ Date _____

27 The stripes on the American flag represent the—

A number of stars on the British flag

B rules in the Flag Code

C number of states today

D original 13 colonies

28 What happened before American leaders passed the first flag resolution?

F Congress passed the Flag Code.

G American leaders met to discuss the flag.

H Francis Scott Key wrote "The Star-Spangled Banner."

J Francis Hopkinson helped design the American flag.

29 In paragraph 4, the word <u>seals</u> means—

A ocean animals

B stamps

C to close

D symbols

30 In which section can the reader find out how to handle the United States Flag?

F An Early American Flag

G The First Official Flag

H Flag Code Rules

J Today's Flag

31 According to the chart, "The Star-Spangled Banner" become the national anthem in—

A 1814

B 1869

C 1931

D 1969

32 According to the chart, which of the following was a member of the original 13 colonies?

F Britain

G Hawaii

H Delaware

J Washington

BE SURE TO MARK YOUR ANSWERS ON THE ANSWER DOCUMENT.

© Houghton Mifflin Harcourt Publishing Company. All rights reserved.

Writing: Revising and Editing

> **Read the introduction and the passage that follows it. Then read each question. Mark your answers on the Answer Document.**

Zachary wrote this story about a girl who overcomes her fear. He would like you to read his story and think about the corrections and improvements he needs to make. Then answer the questions that follow.

The Dance Recital

(1) Cho really, really liked dancing, but she did not like performing in front of an audience. (2) She happily went to dance class every week. (3) She danced around the bushs while her parents gardened. (4) She danced around the house while doing her chores. (5) However, she usually froze when it was time for her end-of-year recital.

(6) She wanted this year's recital to be different. (7) Her dad had an idea. (8) He reminded her that she loved dancing in the garden. (9) He said she should pretend the people in the audience are flowers. (10) That way it would be just like dancing in the garden.

(11) Because Cho practiced her dance every day. (12) She knew the steps by heart. (13) If she could just stop her nerves and move her feat, her dance recital would be perfect.

(14) On the Day of the dance recital, Cho tried to remain calm and cool. (15) However, by the time she changed into her costume for the show, she was not sure she could perform. (16) She remembered what her dad had said. (17) She walked onto the stage, trying to think about flowers. (18) Then she looked out to the audience. (19) Everyone in the audience was holding a flower. (20) The flowers was all from Cho's garden. (21) She saw her father smiling at her from behind a flower. (22) Cho smiled back at him, and then she began to dance.

---

1 What change, if any, should be made in sentence 1?

  A Change *really, really liked* to **loved**

  B Change *did not* to **don't**

  C Change *performing* to **performed**

  D Make no change

2 What change should be made in sentence 3?

  F Change *danced* to **dances**

  G Change *bushs* to **bushes**

  H Change *while* to **during**

  J Change *parents* to **parent's**

3 Which sentence could **BEST** be added after sentence 5?

  A She danced around her room for her stuffed animals.

  B She hoped she would be a ballerina when she grew up.

  C Cho's brother took karate lessons while she was at dance class.

  D Each year she took one look at the audience and ran off the stage.

© Houghton Mifflin Harcourt Publishing Company. All rights reserved.

4 What revision, if any, is needed in sentences 11 and 12?

F Because Cho practiced her dance every day, knew the steps by heart.

G Because Cho practiced her dance every day, she knew the steps by heart.

H Because Cho practiced her dance every day, and she knew the steps by heart.

J No revision is needed.

5 What change should be made in sentence 13?

A Change *could* to **can**

B Change *stop* to **stopped**

C Change *feat* to **feet**

D Change *be* to **been**

6 What change should be made in sentence 14?

F Change *Day* to **day**

G Change the comma to a period

H Change *remain* to **remained**

J Delete *and* after *calm*

7 What change, if any, should be made in sentence 20?

A Change *was* to **were**

B Change *from* to **for**

C Change *Cho's* to **Cho**

D Make no change

GO ON

Name _____ Date _____

Read the introduction and the passage that follows it. Then read each question. Mark your answers on the Answer Document.

Julian is a fourth-grander. He wrote a story about his baby brother. He wants you to help him revise and edit the story. Read Julian's story and think about the changes you would make. Then answer the questions that follow.

Super Brother

(1) My name is Alex, but my new nickname is Super Brother. (2) I have been an older brother for about one year. (3) I just earned my nickname this morning.

(4) I was about to take a drink of orange juice. (5) Suddenly, we herd my baby brother, Grayson, crying. (6) Mom picked him up. (7) She changed his diaper. (8) Then she gently placed him on the carpet so she could wash her hands. (9) That's when Grayson began to cry. (10) Mom whispered to him, but his crying only got worse.

(11) Next, Dad tried to calm Grayson down. (12) Dad picked him up and gave him kiss's on the cheek, but Grayson threw his head back and wailed. (13) My grandmother picked him up and bounced him on her knee, but it had no effect. (14) He was in a very, very bad mood!

Name _____ Date _____

(15) My sister, Allison, took Grayson and began to sing his favorite lullaby. (16) He squeezed his eyes shut, pursed his lips, and screamed even louder. (17) It was unbearable.

(18) Someone had to calm Grayson, but no one was having any luck.

(19) As I walked toward him, I tripped over my own feet. (20) I tried to catch my balance, and both of my armes shot into the air. (21) I didn't fall, but I guess I looked pretty silly. (22) Grayson must have thought so, too, because he stopped crying and started to giggle. (23) His laughter was music to our ears. (24) From now on, my family. (25) They will call me Super Brother. (26) I sure know how to make Grayson laugh!

---

8 Which sentence could **BEST** be added before sentence 4?

  F I'm in fourth grade, and my sister, Allison, is in sixth grade.

  G My sister's name is Allison, but her nickname is Alli.

  H I live in a small house with my mom, my dad, my sister, and my grandmother.

  J It all started as my family was about to sit down for a nice, quiet breakfast.

9 What change should be made in sentence 5?

  A Change *we* to **they**

  B Change *herd* to **heard**

  C Change *crying* to **cried**

  D Change the period to a question mark

© Houghton Mifflin Harcourt Publishing Company. All rights reserved.

Name _____ Date _____

10 What is the **BEST** way to combine sentences 6 and 7?

  F Mom picked him up, changed his diaper.

  G Mom picked him up, she changed his diaper.

  H Mom picked him up and changed his diaper.

  J Mom picked up and she changed him and his diaper.

11 What change should be made in sentence 12?

  A Change *kiss's* to **kisses**

  B Delete the comma after *cheek*

  C Change *but* to **or**

  D Delete *and* after *back*

12 What change, if any, should be made in sentence 14?

  F Change *was* to **were**

  G Change *very, very bad* to **horrible**

  H Change the exclamation mark to a question mark

  J Make no change

13 What change should be made in sentence 20?

  A Change *tried* to **trying**

  B Change *armes* to **arms**

  C Change *shot* to **shut**

  D Change *the* to **an**

14 What revision, if any, is needed in sentences 24 and 25?

  F From now on, my family will call me Super Brother.

  G From now on, my family, they will call me Super Brother.

  H From now on, my family, and they will call me Super Brother.

  J No revision is needed.

GO ON

© Houghton Mifflin Harcourt Publishing Company. All rights reserved.

> **Read the introduction and the passage that follows it. Then read each question. Mark your answers on the Answer Document.**

Katherine's fourth-grade class learned about taste buds. She wrote this report to tell about the interesting facts she learned. She wants you to read her paper and help correct it. Read Katherine's paper and think about the changes she should make. Then answer the questions that follow.

Great Taste

(1) Imagine sinking your teeths into a lemon. (2) Does your mouth pucker just thinking about it? (3) Now think about taking a bite of very, very good watermelon. (4) Can you taste the sweetness? (5) If so, thank your taste buds.

(6) Taste buds are located on your tongue, on the roof of your mouth, and at the back of your throat. (7) If you look in the mirror and stick out your tongue, you can see your taste buds. (8) Right now, you have about 10,000 taste buds. (9) As you get older, you will have fewer.

© Houghton Mifflin Harcourt Publishing Company. All rights reserved.

(10) Scientists know that our taste buds can detect four different tastes—sweet, sour, salty, and bitter. (11) Today, scientists are studying if your taste buds detect other tastes, such as a specific flavor in food.

(12) Your sense of smell is closely linked to your sense of taste. (13) This is why the cent of baking bread can make your mouth water. (14) If you have ever had a stuffy nose. (15) You probably noticed that things did not taste the same. (16) For example, peachs may taste like paper!

(17) You need both your sense of smell and sense of taste to truly enjoy your food. (18) Without them, food would have little flavor. (19) The next time you bite into a delicious sandwich, thank your taste buds for making it so tasty!

---

15 What change should be made in sentence 1?

  A Change *sinking* to **sank**

  B Change *your* to **you're**

  C Change *teeths* to **teeth**

  D Change *into* to **onto**

16 What change should be made in sentence 3?

  F Change *think* to **thinks**

  G Change *bite* to **bites**

  H Insert a comma after *bite*

  J Change *very, very good* to **delicious**

© Houghton Mifflin Harcourt Publishing Company. All rights reserved.

17 Which sentence could **BEST** be added after sentence 7?

A Your back teeth are called molars.

B Pretzels and crackers are salty foods.

C They are the tiny bumps all over your tongue.

D Do you like to taste different kinds of foods?

18 What is the **BEST** way to combine sentences 8 and 9?

F Right now, you have about 10,000 taste buds, as you get older, you will have fewer.

G Right now, you have about 10,000 taste buds, but as you get older, you will have fewer.

H Right now, you have about 10,000 taste buds, or as you get older, you will have fewer.

J Right now, you have about 10,000 taste buds, so as you get older, you will have fewer.

19 What change should be made in sentence 13?

A Change *cent* to **scent**

B Change *baking* to **bake**

C Change *water* to **waters**

D Change the period to a comma

20 What revision, if any, is needed in sentences 14 and 15?

F If you have ever had a stuffy nose, if you probably noticed that things did not taste the same.

G If you have ever had a stuffy nose and probably noticed that things did not taste the same.

H If you have ever had a stuffy nose, you probably noticed that things did not taste the same.

J No revision is needed.

21 What change is needed in sentence 16?

A Delete the comma after *example*

B Change *peachs* to **peaches**

D Change *like* to **likes**

C Change the exclamation point to a question mark

BE SURE TO MARK YOUR ANSWERS ON THE ANSWER DOCUMENT.

Writing: Written Composition

Write a fictional story about a character who helps a friend in need.

Use a separate sheet of paper to plan your composition. Then write your composition on the lined pages that follow.

The information in the box below will help you remember what you should think about when you write your fictional narrative.

REMEMBER—YOU SHOULD

❑ write about a character who helps a friend in need

❑ introduce the setting, characters, and problem at the beginning

❑ use good transitions to make it easy for the reader to follow the order of story events

❑ in the middle of the story, include clues that will help readers understand the ending

❑ try to use correct spelling, capitalization, punctuation, grammar, and sentences

Name _____ Date _____

_____

_____

_____

_____

_____

_____

_____

_____

_____

_____

_____

_____

_____

_____

_____

_____

© Houghton Mifflin Harcourt Publishing Company. All rights reserved.

Name _____ Date _____

_____

_____

_____

_____

_____

_____

_____

_____

_____

_____

_____

_____

_____

_____

© Houghton Mifflin Harcourt Publishing Company. All rights reserved.

Reading

> Read this selection. Then answer the questions that follow it.
> Mark your answers on the Answer Document.

The Protector

1   Eagle sat high in the tree and surveyed the land below. For many years, he had <u>protected</u> the land, and all the animals depended on his great wisdom and strength to keep them safe. Eagle feared nothing, except for <u>people</u>, for he knew they were the only living creatures more powerful than he.

2   As the sun rose on this <u>glorious</u> day, Eagle was pleased because everything was as it should be. Eagle left his perch and flew around the edges of the land. As he flew, he took note of the animals. He also noticed Farmer, tending to the animals. <u>Although</u> Farmer took care of animals and appeared to be kindhearted, Eagle still was careful to stay far away from him. After all, the farmer was a person.

3   During the day Eagle kept a watchful eye on the animals. Despite the sweltering temperature, Eagle remained alert all day. In the early afternoon, Deer came to Eagle and told him of a strange object she had discovered in the woods. Eagle agreed to come <u>inspect</u> it and followed Deer as she led the way.

4   Soon Deer and Eagle reached the <u>unusual</u> object. It was made of a shiny metal and had sharp edges. Eagle recognized it at once, explaining to Deer that it was a trap. Deer was confused, so Eagle explained that people sometimes use traps to catch animals. Eagle told Deer to leave and warn the other animals about the trap. He would <u>decide</u> how to get rid of it so it could not hurt any of the animals.

5   Eagle flew high into the sky because he did his best thinking while flying. As he was trying to figure out what to do, he noticed Mouse walking near the trap. Mouse had his head in the clouds. Eagle's response was <u>automatic</u>. He let out a sharp "wee-aaaa" and flew toward Mouse. Eagle struck Mouse and knocked him out of the way. The trap clamped down tightly on Eagle's leg, and he let out a piercing screech.

6   Farmer was working nearby and heard Eagle's cry. His animals heard the cry, too, for they became agitated. Farmer patted the animals and spoke to them soothingly. Then he went into the woods to see what had happened to Eagle.

7   Farmer found Eagle caught in the trap. Eagle's heart raced as he wondered if Farmer was the one who set the trap. Did this person intend to cause him harm? Farmer spoke in a velvety voice, assuring Eagle that he was there to help. Farmer freed Eagle and took the trap back to his farm, where he disposed of it. Eagle flew away from the woods and was happy that he was not harmed.

8   The next day, Eagle surveyed the land. He noticed Farmer working in the middle of the hot day. Farmer wiped his sweaty brow often. The next time Eagle flew by he saw that Farmer was sitting in the shade of an <u>immense</u> stone wall. Eagle heard a low, rumbling sound that only his keen ears could sense. Suddenly, Eagle dove towards the Farmer. He swooped down and <u>yanked</u> Farmer's hat from his head. Farmer stood up at once and ran after Eagle, who dropped the hat on the ground.

9   Farmer was confused by Eagle's actions. He wondered why Eagle would take his hat after he had treated Eagle with kindness. Just then, Farmer heard a loud noise behind him. He turned around as the old wall came tumbling down where he had been sitting just moments before. Farmer understood Eagle's selfless action and waved to Eagle in thanks.

© Houghton Mifflin Harcourt Publishing Company. All rights reserved.

1 Look at the word <u>protected</u> in paragraph 1. Then complete this analogy: <u>Rescued</u> is to <u>saved</u> as <u>protected</u> is to—

A taken

B found

C guarded

D trapped

2 How is Eagle different from the other animals?

F He is larger and older.

G He can speak to people.

H He can speak to animals.

J He is wiser and stronger.

3 In paragraph 2, the word <u>glorious</u> means—

A cold

B usual

C beautiful

D frightening

4 At the beginning of the story, the reader can tell that Eagle—

F does not trust people

G wants to trick Farmer

H feels sorry for Farmer's animals

J has never seen a person before

5 Which word is an antonym for the word <u>unusual</u> in paragraph 4?

A Bright

B Ordinary

C Strange

D Dangerous

6 Eagle first flies away from the trap because he—

F does not want to be caught

G wants Mouse to learn a lesson

H does not want to frighten Deer

J needs to think of a way to get rid of it

7 When the author says Mouse "had his head in the clouds" in paragraph 5, this means Mouse was—

A trying to fly

B looking for Eagle

C not paying attention

D climbing a tree

8 In paragraph 5, the word <u>automatic</u> means—

F like a car

G very brave

H carefully planned

J done without thinking

9 Look at the chart below and use it to answer the question.

Story Event	Conclusion
• Eagle watches over all the animals in the land. • Eagle knows the shiny object is a trap. • Eagle tells Deer to stay away from the trap.	Eagle is brave and wise.
• Farmer takes care of his animals. • Farmer speaks soothingly to his animals to calm them. • Farmer frees Eagle from the trap.	

Which sentence belongs in the empty box?

A Farmer is lazy.

B Farmer is kind.

C Farmer set the trap.

D Farmer does not like Eagle.

10 How are Mouse and Deer alike?

F They both try to free Eagle.

G They both like the Farmer.

H They both need help from Eagle.

J They both are puzzled by the trap.

11 In paragraph 8, what does the word <u>immense</u> mean?

A Huge

B Old

C Gray

D Broken

GO ON

© Houghton Mifflin Harcourt Publishing Company. All rights reserved.

12 In paragraph 8, the word <u>yanked</u> means—

F pulled

G stole

H dropped

J slid

13 Eagle takes Farmer's hat to—

A play a joke on Farmer

B let Farmer know he is angry

C show that he is faster than Farmer

D make Farmer move away from the wall

14 The author most likely wrote this story to—

F describe forest animals

G tell an entertaining story

H give interesting facts about Eagles

J make people want to protect Eagles

15 Which of these shows the correct way to stress the syllables of the word <u>people</u>?

A PEO • PLE

B PEO • ple

C peo • PLE

D peo • ple

16 Which of these shows the correct way to divide the word <u>although</u> into syllables?

F alth • ough

G a • lthough

H alt • hough

J al • though

17 Which of these shows the correct way to divide the word <u>inspect</u> into syllables?

A ins • pect

B in • spect

C insp • ect

D i • nspect

18 Which word has the same beginning syllable as the word decide?

F Deeply

G Dealing

H Delicious

J Dentist

GO ON

Read the next two selections. Then answer the questions that follow them. Mark your answers on the Answer Document.

Jessie's Idea

1   I have just seen the movie *Jessie's Idea*. I think that everyone else should see it, too. Ten-year-old Caroline Lyons plays Jessie. In the movie, Jessie wants to prevent pollution around the world. She turns her idea into her fourth grade science fair experiment. After winning the science fair, Jessie tries to share her plan with world leaders. Sadly, because of her age, no one takes her seriously.

2   Jessie refuses to give up. She explains her idea to anyone who will listen, including a <u>wealthy</u> person named Mr. Melin. Played by Brian Turner, Mr. Melin takes the idea as his own. He uses his power and money to set the plan in motion. Mr. Melin begins appearing on television and in magazines, promoting "his" idea for the end of pollution. People wrongly see him as a hero.

3   Jessie is excited to see her idea put into action, but she wishes she had not shared it with Mr. Melin. With help from her <u>teacher</u>, Ms. Lane, played by Felicia Nance, Jessie goes to the White House to set the record straight. However, Mr. Melin refuses to go away. He tries to kidnap Jessie and Ms. Lane in order to keep his secret. Even though you know Jessie will <u>triumph</u> in the end, the movie is still fun to watch.

4   Movie watchers will enjoy the <u>action</u>-packed story and the star cast. It is a drama, but it has many <u>humorous</u> parts, too. Most importantly, if you see this movie, you might believe that the future belongs to the children.

Inside a Movie Studio

1   Hundreds of movies have been filmed at the Stars Movie Studio. The studio has recently started providing daily tours for the public. Here's what visitors can expect to see there.

2   The movie studio is huge! To get around its 200 acres, visitors ride on a tram, which looks a lot like a long golf cart. As they ride through the studio grounds, a tour guide points out different areas.

3   The first stop is a sound stage. On the outside, a sound stage looks like a large barn. There may even be cows inside! Many movie scenes are shot in a sound stage. The walls of a sound stage keep outside sounds out of the building. Workers build a set inside the sound stage. The set may be an office building or even a village. Once the set is ready, the director guides the <u>actors</u> through scenes while camera people film the action.

4   One sound stage is an underwater stage. It's an <u>enormous</u> swimming pool for shooting underwater scenes. Do you remember when Mr. Melin's car drove into the river in *Jessie's Idea*? That scene was shot in the Stars underwater stage.

5   Visitors will also see the studio's back lot, which is a street lined with houses. It looks like a street anywhere in the country. It has been used in many movies. However, if you walk around to the side of the houses, you will see that they are not real! Only the front of each house was built. The back lot also has woods. Look closely and you will see that the trees and boulders are on wheels so they can be moved easily.

6   The last stop on the tour is a museum where visitors can see <u>genuine</u> props from movies filmed at Stars. For example, they might see the coat Caroline Lyons wore in *Jessie's Idea*. The most exciting part of the tour might just be seeing the real actors at work. You may be lucky enough to see one in action, but you are not allowed to ask for an <u>autograph</u>.

© Houghton Mifflin Harcourt Publishing Company. All rights reserved.

Use "Jessie's Idea" to answer questions 19–24.

19 Which statement from the selection is a fact?

A *I think that everyone else should see it, too.*

B *Ten-year-old Caroline Lyons plays Jessie.*

C *Even though you know Jessie will triumph in the end, the movie is still fun to watch.*

D *Movie watchers will enjoy the action-packed story and the star cast.*

20 In paragraph 2, the word <u>wealthy</u> is used to let the reader know that Mr. Melin is—

F angry

G rich

H healthy

J mean

21 In paragraph 3, when the author says Jessie goes to the White House "to set the record straight," this means Jessie—

A listens to a record

B makes a recording of her voice

C places records in a straight line

D wants to correct a misunderstanding

22 In paragraph 3, the word <u>triumph</u> means—

F succeed

G disappoint

H race

J experiment

23 The reader can tell that *Jessie's Idea* takes place—

A in ancient times

B in outer space

C in modern times

D in another country

24 What does the word <u>humorous</u> mean in paragraph 4?

F Long

G Huge

H Funny

J Scary

GO ON

© Houghton Mifflin Harcourt Publishing Company. All rights reserved.

Use "Inside a Movie Studio" to answer questions 25–30.

25 The author most likely wrote this selection to—

A explain how to film an underwater scene

B make readers interested in making movies

C tell readers how movie directors use the sound stage

D describe some interesting parts of Stars Movie Studio

26 Which statement from the selection is an opinion?

F *Hundreds of movies have been filmed at the Stars Movie Studio.*

G *The walls of a sound stage keep outside sounds out of the building.*

H *Visitors will also see the studio's back lot, which is a street lined with houses.*

J *The most exciting part of the tour might just be seeing the real actors at work.*

27 Which word is an antonym for the word <u>enormous</u> in paragraph 4?

A Tiny

B Clear

C Huge

D Warm

28 What does the word <u>genuine</u> mean in paragraph 6?

F Tall

G Actual

H Important

J Impressive

29 In paragraph 6, what does the word <u>autograph</u> mean?

A Picture

B Present

C Signature

D Handshake

30 What generalization can the reader make from the article?

F Movies never have real houses in them.

G Movies can only be filmed in a sound stage.

H All movies are filmed in an underwater stage.

J A sound stage can be used for almost any type of movie scene.

GO ON

© Houghton Mifflin Harcourt Publishing Company. All rights reserved.

Use "Jessie's Idea" and "Inside a Movie Studio" to answer questions 31–35.

31 What can the reader tell about the movie *Jessie's Idea* from both selections?

A It was difficult to film.

B It was filmed entirely underwater.

C It was filmed at the Stars movie studio.

D It was filmed on a back lot.

32 The reader can tell that the authors of both selections—

F are movie critics

G know movie actors

H work in a movie studio

J saw the movie *Jessie's Idea*

33 Which of the following shows the correct way to stress the syllables in the word actors?

A AC • TORS

B AC • tors

C ac • TORS

D ac • tors

34 Which of the following shows the correct way to stress the syllables in the word action?

F ac • tion

G ac • TION

H AC • tion

J AC • TION

35 Which of the following shows the correct way to divide the word teacher into syllables?

A te • acher

B teach • er

C teac • her

D tea • cher

BE SURE TO MARK YOUR ANSWERS ON THE ANSWER DOCUMENT. STOP

© Houghton Mifflin Harcourt Publishing Company. All rights reserved.

Name _____ Date _____

Writing: Revising and Editing

> Read the introduction and the passage that follows it. Then read each
> question. Mark your answers on the Answer Document.

*Carlin wrote this paper about a time when he was surprised. He would like
you to read his paper and suggest the corrections and improvements he should
make. When you are finished reading, answer the questions that follow.*

The Best Surprise

(1) Last Wednesday began like any other ordinary day. (2) When my

alarm clock woke me up at 6:30 A.M., I stretched and crawled out of bed.

(3) My dog, Tilley, let out a houl. (4) Then she leapt up to greet me with

a big lick. (5) I put on my favorite slippers and went into the kitchen to

eat breakfast. (6) That's when I witnessed it. (7) There was snow on the

ground! (8) No two snowflakes are exactly alike. (9) It looked like someone

had thrown a giant white blanket across our lawn.

© Houghton Mifflin Harcourt Publishing Company. All rights reserved.

(10) So I live in Central Texas, I do not see much snow. (11) In fact, I can only recall seeing it snow one other time. (12) You can imagine how excited I was to see real snow!

(13) Mom entered the kitchen with my younger brother. (14) She informed me that school was cancelled today because of the snow. (15) All of us eager to go out to play, so we munched a quick breakfast and got dressed. (16) We put on our warmest coats and hats, and took the gloves and scarves out from the bottom of our drawers. (17) Then we moved outside to play in the fresh snow. (18) They made snowballs, a snow person, and a snow fort. (19) It was a really fun way to spend the day. (20) The snow will be a great surprise!

GO ON ➤

© Houghton Mifflin Harcourt Publishing Company. All rights reserved.

1 What change should be made in sentence 3?

   A Change *dog* to **dogs**

   B Delete the comma before *Tilley*

   C Insert a period after *Tilley*

   D Change *houl* to **howl**

2 Which sentence does **NOT** belong in this paper?

   F Sentence 6

   G Sentence 7

   H Sentence 8

   J Sentence 9

3 What change should be made in sentence 10?

   A Change *So* to **Since**

   B Change *Central Texas* to **central texas**

   C Delete the comma after *Texas*

   D Change *much* to **many**

4 What change should be made in sentence 15?

   F Insert **were** before *eager*

   G Delete the comma after *play*

   H Delete *so* before *munched*

   J Change *dressed* to **dress**

5 What is the **BEST** way to revise sentence 17?

   A Change *Then* to **After**

   B Change *we* to **us**

   C Change *moved* to **dashed**

   D Change *fresh* to **freshly**

6 What change, if any, should be made in sentence 18?

   F Change *They* to **We**

   G Delete the comma after *person*

   H Delete the comma after *snowballs*

   J Make no change

7 What change, if any, should be made in sentence 20?

   A Change *The* to **Those**

   B Change *will be* to **was**

   C Change the exclamation mark to a question mark

   D Make no change

GO ON

> **Read the introduction and the passage that follows it. Then read each question. Mark your answers on the Answer Document.**

Juan is a fourth grader. He wrote this report about a place he would like to visit. He wants you to help him with the revising and editing before he turns the report in to his teacher. Read the report and think about the changes he should make. Then answer the questions that follow.

Yellowstone National Park

(1) Yellowstone National Park located in parts of Wyoming, Montana, and Idaho. (2) The park was organized in 1872. (3) It was our country's first national park. (4) It was set up to protect the wilderness so that future generations could enjoy the wilderness. (5) In a national park, people cannot farm, hunt, or change the land in any way. (6) One day, I hope to visit Yellowstone to go camping, fishing, and hiking.

(7) Yellowstone is known for geysers. (8) There are more than 100 of these at Yellowstone, Old Faithful is the most famous one. (9) It goes off once every hour and a half, shooting boiling water more than 100 feet in the air! (10) That is a sight I hope to see one day.

(11) There are also hot springs at the park. (12) Underground, water is heated as it comes into contact with hot rock. (13) The heated water works its way to the surface where it formed pools of hot water. (14) The hot springs often look yellow, orange, and green because of the rocks, bacteria, and algae.

(15) Visitors to Yellowstone can also see wild animals. (16) Elk, bison, sheep wolves, and even grizzly bears all live at the park. (17) You are most likely to see it during the early morning or early evening hours when it is the animals' feeding time.

---

8 What change, if any, should be made in sentence 1?

  F Change *National Park* to **national park**

  G Insert **is** after *Park*

  H Delete the comma after Montana

  J Make no change

9 What is the **BEST** way to rewrite sentence 4?

  A It was set up, to protect the wilderness, so that future generations could enjoy the wilderness.

  B Set it up to protect the wilderness so that future generations could enjoy it.

  C It was set up to protect it so that future generations could enjoy the wilderness.

  D It was set up to protect the wilderness so that future generations could enjoy it.

GO ON

10 Which sentence should be added after sentence 7?

  F People can watch Old Faithful erupt on the Internet.

  G Millions of people visit Yellowstone National Park each year.

  H Most of Yellowstone National Park is in the state of Wyoming.

  J A geyser is like a fountain that shoots hot water into the air.

11 What change, if any, should be made in sentence 8?

  A Delete the comma after *Yellowstone*

  B Insert **and** after the comma

  C Change *most* to **mostly**

  D Make no change

12 What change, if any, should be made in sentence 13?

  F Change *works* to **work**

  G Change *its* to **it's**

  H Change *formed* to **forms**

  J Make no change

13 What change, if any, should be made in sentence 16?

  A Insert a comma after *sheep*

  B Change *wolves* to **wolfs**

  C Change *live* to **lives**

  D Make no change

14 What change should be made in sentence 17?

  F Change *likely* to **possibly**

  G Change *it* to **them**

  H Change *hours* to **ours**

  J Insert a comma after *animals'*

GO ON

© Houghton Mifflin Harcourt Publishing Company. All rights reserved.

Read the introduction and the passage that follows it. Then read each
question. Mark your answers on the Answer Document.

*Jordan wrote this paper that includes fun facts she learned about frogs and
toads. She wants you to read her paper and think about the changes she
needs to make to improve it. When you finish reading, answer the questions
that follow.*

Interesting Facts About Frogs and Toads

(1) Imagine watching the weather report on the evening news. (2) The

meteorologist predict an 80 percent chance of rain the following day.

(3) You would expect it to rain. (4) You might even get out your umbrella

to be prepared. (5) Would you ever suspect that you might need to put on a

hard hat? (6) That's because it could potentially rain frogs! (7) No this isn't

a scene from a fantasy movie. (8) It sounds wierd, but it can actually rain

frogs. (9) There have been many reports of rain containing frogs.

(10) You might wonder how this could happen. (11) High wind or a tornado can passed over a pond or other body of water and pick up frogs, fish, and other marine animals. (12) These animals will then tumble from the sky in another location.

(13) You may have heard that frogs and toads can give you warts. (14) Have you wondered if this is true? (15) Have no fear because it is only a myth. (16) A human virus causes warts. (17) You cannot get them from frogs or toads. (18) This myth may have started because a toad having bumpy skin. (19) These bumps resemble warts, or they are there to help conceal a toad from its enemies. (20) A frog has damp, slick skin to keep you moist. (21) Even though you cannot get a wart from a frog or toad, you should always wash your hands after touching one.

GO ON

15 What change, if any, should be made in sentence 2?

   A Insert **has** before *predict*

   B Change *predict* to **predicts**

   C Insert a comma after *rain*

   D Make no change

16 What change, if any, should be made in sentence 7?

   F Insert a comma after *No*

   G Change *scene* to **seen**

   H Change the period to a question mark

   J Make no change

17 What change should be made in sentence 8?

   A Change *sounds* to **sound**

   B Change *wierd* to **weird**

   C Change *but* to **and**

   D Change *actually* to **actual**

18 What change should be made in sentence 11?

   F Change *or* to **and**

   G Change *can* to **could**

   H Change *passed* to **pass**

   J Insert a comma after *water*

19 What change should be made in sentence 18?

   A Change *This* to **These**

   B Change *started* to **starts**

   C Change *because* to **although**

   D Change *having* to **has**

20 What change should be made in sentence 19?

   F Delete the comma after *warts*

   G Change *or* to **and**

   H Change *are* to **is**

   J Change *its* to **it's**

21 What change, if any, should be made in sentence 20?

   A Delete the comma after *dump*

   B Change *slick* to **slicker**

   C Insert a comma after *skin*

   D Change *you* to **it**

BE SURE TO MARK YOUR ANSWERS ON THE ANSWER DOCUMENT.

Writing: Written Composition

Read the story below and respond to the prompt that follows it.

My Aunt Julia

My Aunt Julia has always been my hero. When she smiles, her whole face lights up. It is one of her secret weapons. With that smile, and her "can-do" energy, she can get almost anything done. Now she's the neighborhood hero!

Not far from our neighborhood, there was a city block that was a big mess. Some buildings had been knocked down, but the area hadn't been cleaned up. Hunks of concrete, big steel bars, and broken wooden beams covered the ground. During the next weeks and months, garbage started piling up. One day, workers came and put up an ugly fence.

Aunt Julia believed the people in her neighborhood didn't deserve this eyesore and decided to do something about it. First, she made phone calls to find out who owned the land. She learned that the land belonged to the city. Next, she called the mayor's office to find out what he would do to clean it up. His assistant told her that the city had big plans for the property.

Weeks passed. Aunt Julia waited patiently. Nothing happened. Instead of giving up, Aunt Julia decided this time she would write a letter to the mayor asking for action. She knew that you have to keep trying if you want to succeed. Aunt Julia also decided to get some support from the neighbors by having them sign her letter. She talked all of the neighbors into joining her. Aunt Julia did a lot of smiling that day.

The mayor's office did not answer her letter. More time went by, and still nothing happened. Now Aunt Julia was even more determined. She called the local newspaper. The newspaper wrote a front-page article about how the mayor had done nothing to fix up the block in Aunt Julia's neighborhood. Within a week all of the garbage, concrete, metal, and wood was gone. The ugly fence was gone, too.

Soon after that, the mayor's office called Aunt Julia and asked if she had any ideas for the block. They were putting her in charge of it! Of course, Aunt Julia already had a plan. First, she went to the local Garden Club and asked them for help planting trees, shrubs, and flowers. She went to businesses in the neighborhood and asked them to donate materials and other supplies. With the help from the neighborhood, Aunt Julia turned the property into a beautiful park.

As a final bonus, Aunt Julia brought lots of people together who used to be strangers, even though they lived close to each other. Some of them even became good friends.

My Aunt Julia always says, "You can get anything done if you try hard enough." After watching her, I definitely have to agree.

> Do you think Aunt Julia is a hero? Write a response to literature composition that tells why or why not.

Use a separate sheet of paper to plan your composition. Then write your composition on the lined pages that follow.

The information in the box below will help you remember what you should think about when you write your composition.

REMEMBER—YOU SHOULD

❏ write to tell whether you think Aunt Julia is a hero or not

❏ write an opening that uses words from the question and states your opinion

❏ give strong reasons for your opinion and support your opinion with evidence from the story

❏ write an ending that sums up your opinion

❏ try to use correct spelling, capitalization, punctuation, grammar, and sentences

Name _____ Date _____

_____

_____

_____

_____

_____

_____

_____

_____

_____

_____

_____

_____

_____

_____

_____

_____

_____

_____

_____

_____

_____

_____

_____

_____

_____

_____

_____

_____

_____

© Houghton Mifflin Harcourt Publishing Company. All rights reserved.

Reading

> **Read this selection. Then answer the questions that follow it.**
> **Mark your answer on the Answer Document.**

Digging For Africa's
Lost Dinosaurs

by Lesley Reed

1 "Paleontology is more than science," says world-famous <u>paleontologist</u> Paul Sereno. "You get to travel, meet new people, and have adventures." He should know—he's spent 15 years on one of the greatest dinosaur adventures ever.

2 For millions of years, dinosaur fossils have lain untouched in Africa's Sahara desert—that is, until Sereno decided to brave the extreme heat and harsh travel. Before Sereno went to Africa, very few dinosaurs had been discovered on that continent. Sereno knew that the secret to finding lots of new fossils was to go where no one else had gone. But crossing the Sahara to search for fossils was not going to be easy.

3 On Sereno's first expedition, he and his team crossed 1,500 miles of desert. They climbed over sand dunes the size of mountains. When they arrived in the country of Niger, the government wouldn't allow them to dig. And robbers were such a problem that the team needed an armed guard. After working everything out, they had only a short time to do their work. But they discovered a dinosaur gold mine. Sereno and his team found one of the richest dinosaur "beds" in Africa.

Paul Sereno discovering the thighbone of the *Jobaria*, a dinosaur that weighed about 20 tons.

GO ON

© Houghton Mifflin Harcourt Publishing Company. All rights reserved.

Workers and others crowd around the skeleton of a
Suchomimus, which may have been 36 feet long and 12
feet high.

4   Within days, they found the remains of a new meat-eating dinosaur.
Bigger and faster than Allosaurus, they named it *Afrovenator*, for
"African hunter." They found and named many others. *Suchomimus*
had a sail on its back and a long crocodile-like snout used for catching
fish. (The Sahara once had a lot of water.) *Nigersauras* had 600 teeth.
And *Sarcosuchus* was a crocodile-like dinosaur as long as a bus.

5   There are many challenges to working in the
Sahara. With temperatures over 120 degrees,
it's easy to feel like a cookie baking in an oven.
Fortunately, Sereno doesn't mind. "I adapt to
heat like a lizard," he says. And he drinks lots
of water.

6   Where does he get water in the desert? He
and his team carry it with them. From medical
supplies to freeze-dried ice cream bars, the
team takes whatever they need. On one trip,
they carried 600 pounds of pasta and 4,000
gallons of water.

7   All the effort is worth it. "Every dinosaur
we've found in Africa is new," says Sereno. "Not
one is the same as those on other continents.
That's why it's thrilling—it's a lost world."

Measuring the length of a
Sarcosuchus, the "Super
Croc," which was about
40 feet long.

GO ON ➡

1 In paragraph 1, the suffix *-ologist* in the word <u>paleontologist</u> suggests the word means one who—

A studies

B experiences life

C believes in science

D travels the world

2 Why had few dinosaur fossils been discovered in the Sahara over time?

F The heat had destroyed most fossils.

G Not many dinosaurs lived in Africa.

H The area is a difficult place to travel in and dig.

J The area was protected by armed guards.

3 How does the article say that the Sahara today is different than it used to be long ago?

A Today it is hot and dry, but it used to have a lot of water.

B Today it is home to dinosaurs, but it never was before.

C It once was an easy place to search, but not anymore.

D It once had mountains, but now it is flat.

4 What happened right after Sereno and his team found their first dinosaur bed in Africa?

F They had to climb over sand dunes the size of mountains.

G They learned the government of Niger would not let them dig.

H They found the remains of a new meat-eating dinosaur.

J They discovered a dinosaur that had a sail on its back.

5 The author says that Sereno's team found a dinosaur "gold mine" because—

A the fossils had been buried with treasures

B the team had to dig very deep for what they found

C the fossils they found were numerous

D the team risked being trapped inside their digs

6 Why did Sereno need armed guards for his digs?

F His digs were against the law.

G There were problems with robbers.

H The Sahara was crowded with people.

J There was a threat of wild animals.

GO ON

© Houghton Mifflin Harcourt Publishing Company. All rights reserved.

> **Read this selection. Then answer the questions that follow it.**
> **Mark your answer on the Answer Document.**

Being a Good Friend

1   Ellie hummed to herself as she waited for Jada at their usual meeting place, the oak tree by the traffic light. The two classmates had been best friends since they were introduced to each other in kindergarten. They met at that spot almost every day after school was dismissed, and then, laughing and chatting, they accompanied each other for the walk home.

2   Ellie's apartment building was the first stop. The girls would arrive there, have some refreshments, and stay for awhile to play and to visit.

3   As Ellie waited this afternoon, she scanned the lawn for four-leaf clovers that she could give to Jada, because Jada considered them a sign of good luck.

4   Ellie was concentrating so hard on her search that she didn't notice Jada had passed by. When she looked up, she saw Jada walking with Katie, whose family had just moved there from out of state.

5   Ellie scrambled to her feet and reached for her knapsack. She called out to Jada, but her friend acted as if she had not heard. Ellie raced down the street until she caught up with Jada.

6   "Hey, did you forget about me?" Ellie asked.

7   Jada and Katie exchanged glances. Then Jada looked coolly at Ellie.

8   "I thought I saw you sitting there, but I wasn't sure," she said.

9   "Why didn't you say anything?"

10   "You were so busy picking at the grass, I didn't want to disturb you," Jada said.

11   Her new friend giggled, and made no effort to hide her amusement. Ellie felt embarrassed and confused at the idea of Jada making fun of

© Houghton Mifflin Harcourt Publishing Company. All rights reserved.

Name _____ Date _____

her. She turned away abruptly and walked to her house alone. After closing the door behind her, she peered out the window as the two girls walked together past her house.

12   The next day, Ellie wondered if Jada would call for her on her way to school. However, when she saw Jada approaching with her new friend, Ellie hid in the living room until they were out of sight. Later she trudged to school by herself, feeling more alone than she had ever felt in her life.

13   After the dismissal bell sounded, Ellie waited again by the oak tree. This time, she didn't search for clovers. Instead, she pretended to be fascinated by her math textbook. When she heard giggling, she knew that Jada and her new friend were nearby. Again, Jada did not stop to give a greeting, so Ellie continued to read as if there were nothing else in the world except that textbook. Inside, however, she felt very sad.

14   As the days passed, Ellie no longer waited for Jada after school by the oak tree. Ellie missed her friend, but she didn't know how to attract her attention, so she decided to just leave it alone.

15   One Friday, Ellie noticed Jada leaning up against the bark of the oak tree. She walked over and said hello. Jada smiled shyly.

16   "I've been such a bad friend," said Jada regretfully. "I'm sorry."

17   "It's okay," answered Ellie, though the expression on her face showed that it really wasn't.

18   "It was interesting to meet Katie," Jada went on. "We have a lot of the same interests, you know. But I know that was no excuse to treat you poorly. Now Katie has found a new friend, and I think I know just how you felt. Ellie, can you forgive me?"

19   When Ellie said yes this time, she meant it sincerely.

20   "I have something for you," said Jada. She displayed a four-leaf clover, which she had carefully glued to a hand-painted cardboard rectangle. Plastic wrap protected the leaves.

21   "I found it yesterday in my front yard," Jada went on. "I know it's good luck, since you are still my friend!"

7 This story first takes place—

A on a neighborhood street

B in Ellie's living room

C at the bus stop

D in Jada's front yard

8 In paragraph 16, what does the word <u>regretfully</u> mean?

F With a lack of awareness

G With deep anger over someone else's actions

H With great confidence in oneself

J With a sense of sadness or disappointment

9 Jada refuses to answer when Ellie calls to her because she—

A is too interested in her math textbook

B has been trying to hide from Ellie

C does not realize Ellie is there

D is with Katie and ignoring Ellie

10 Which event helps Jada realize how poorly she has treated Ellie?

F Ellie's family moves to another state

G Ellie tells her how hurt she is

H Katie treats Jada the same way

J Katie tells Jada she has been mean to Ellie

11 At the end of the story, Jada gives Ellie—

A a painting she had made

B her math textbook

C a four-leaf clover

D a snack they had once enjoyed together

12 Which sentence best describes the theme of the story?

F A good friend would never do anything bad to you.

G It is best to not expect much from your friends so you don't get hurt.

H It is too hard for anyone to be a good friend all of the time.

J A good friend knows when he or she is being a bad friend.

© Houghton Mifflin Harcourt Publishing Company. All rights reserved.

Name _____ Date _____

Read this selection. Then answer the questions that follow it.
Mark your answer on the Answer Document.

Good Health

1 What's so great about exercise? Even if the thought of jogging around a track, jumping rope, or getting hot and dirty makes you shudder, there are ways that working out can still be fun. You might enjoy a game like volleyball, or maybe you ride your bicycle with friends. You could also get moving through the daily responsibility of walking your dog.

2 These are all ways to work out, or exercise. Exercise is a must in order to gain and preserve good health. It strengthens your body, gives you more energy, and even makes you feel happier.

3 When you exercise, you use your muscles. This makes them stronger, including muscles deep inside the body, such as your heart. The job of the heart muscle is to pump blood throughout the body. The blood contains oxygen, which reaches every part of the body by <u>coursing</u> through blood vessels. A strong heart gets the job done more effectively, and with less effort. It certainly is worthwhile to strengthen that muscle.

4 When you are healthy, you feel like you have more energy. Energy is the power to move around. A healthy body does not have to work as hard to move, and it does not get tired as quickly.

5 Another plus about exercise is that is makes you feel good. Exercise causes the body to produce a kind of chemical in the brain that calms you, and raises your spirits too. This chemical change is in addition to the good feelings you get from being stronger and having more energy.

6 Eating right is another way to stay healthy. Breakfast is very important if you make it a healthy one. It provides power to your body and to your brain.

7 It's easier to choose healthy foods if you know what you need. Children generally need about a cup and a half of fruit and a cup and a half of vegetables every day. You should drink between four and eight glasses of water and juice each day.

GO ON ➡

© Houghton Mifflin Harcourt Publishing Company. All rights reserved.

Name _____ Date _____

8   The final ingredient for good health is to get enough rest. Growing children need an average of nine hours of sleep every night. When the body is asleep it repairs itself.

9   The body is like a machine. If you take good care of it, it can work well for a long time.

---

13 This article is mainly about—

  A what happens to an unhealthy body

  B different ways to have a healthy body

  C what children should eat and drink

  D the importance of exercise

14 In paragraph 3, what does the word <u>coursing</u> mean?

  F Filtering out

  G Dripping into

  H Carrying back

  J Passing through

15 Sleep helps the body by—

  A giving it more oxygen

  B allowing it to repair itself

  C raising its spirits

  D pumping blood through it

16 Why does the author say that the body is "like a machine"?

  F It is very powerful.

  G It works all the time.

  H To get it to work well, you must take good care of it.

  J It does what you need it to do automatically, with no effort from you.

17 A healthy body is different from an unhealthy body because a healthy body—

  A has more energy

  B has less energy

  C never gets tired

  D gets tired quickly

GO ON

© Houghton Mifflin Harcourt Publishing Company. All rights reserved.

Name _____ Date _____

**Read this selection. Then answer the questions that follow it.
Mark your answer on the Answer Document.**

A Tree Needs a Special Place

by Lyda Williamson
illustrated by Laura Jacobsen

1   Oscar leaped up onto the porch and <u>bounded</u> into the house. He unzipped his backpack, pulled out a plastic bag, and ran to find *Mamá*.

2   "Mamá, look!" shouted Oscar. He opened the bag to reveal a baby tree, roots and all. "We got them at school for Arbor Day."

3   "How exciting!" said Mamá.

4   Oscar looked at the tree. "But I don't know where to plant it."

5   Mamá smiled. "It needs a special place. When we moved here from Mexico, I was a little girl. I didn't have any friends. Our new house had a big backyard with an oak tree. My father hung a swing from it, and I'd swing for hours. One day, a little girl came over and asked if she could swing with me. It was Claudia."

6   Oscar nodded. Claudia was Mamá's best friend. "Maybe someday this tree will grow big enough for a swing," he said. "I'll go show *Abuelito* and *Abuelita*!"

7   Oscar sprinted downstairs to his grandparents' apartment.

8   Abuelito, Oscar's grandfather, opened the door. "¡*Hola*, Oscar!"

9   "Look, Abuelito! I got a tree at school for Arbor Day," Oscar said. "But I don't know where to plant it. We don't have a big backyard like Mamá did."

10   Abuelito smoothed back his graying hair. "No, but we'll find a place for it," he said. He squatted down to look at the tree. "Back in Mexico, the sun is so strong at midday that everyone must take a break. A huge paloverde tree grew at the edge of our cornfield. I loved to rest in its shade."

Name _____ Date _____

11   Abuelita laughed. "I can still picture you there!" She put her hand on Oscar's shoulder. "Let me tell you about my favorite trees," she said. "My mamá loved to make *agua de limón*. It's like lemonade, but it's made with limes. Lime trees grew everywhere in my town! Mamá would send me out to pick the limes, then she'd let me stir the water, juice, and sugar. We'd use colorful straws to sip our cool green drinks."

12   "Mmmm, sounds good," said Oscar.

13   "I'll make it for you sometime," said Abuelita. "Now go find a spot to plant *your* tree."

14   "I will!" said Oscar. He raced up the steps and out the front door. Just as he stepped onto the porch, *Papá* pulled up in his car.

15   "What do you have there?" asked Papá.

16   Oscar showed him the tree.

17   Papá smiled. "When I was a boy in Michigan, my father would always make guacamole with avocados from the store.

18   Oscar nodded. He liked the tasty green dip.

19   "He'd mix it up and talk about Mexico. One time he saved the avocado seed. We put it in water. Every day, I watched it. Soon a tiny green sprout appeared. It became a baby tree. We nursed it along, then planted it in the ground."

20   "Did avocados grow on it, Papá?" asked Oscar.

21   "No, it couldn't survive the cold winter," Papa said. "But I'll always remember that special time with my father."

22   Oscar's sister walked up the sidewalk toward them.

23   "Magdalena, look!" Oscar held up the tree. "But I need a place to plant it."

24   "Let's see," said Magdalena. "At our old house, when you were a baby, a huge poplar tree grew near our sidewalk. It was taller than every other tree around. Wherever I was in town, I could always see our tree high above everything else."

Name _____ Date _____

25   Oscar glanced at the wide strip of grass between their sidewalk and the street. It was the perfect place! "Thanks, Magdalena—I'm going to plant my tree right here."

26   The sun was beginning to set. By now, the rest of Oscar's family had come outside to see where Oscar would plant his tree.

27   Oscar read the planting directions. "'Every fall this sugar maple will turn a brilliant red-orange. To plant it, dig a hole twice the size of the roots. Place the roots in the hole, and fill it with dirt. Water the tree often for the first year.'"

28   Abuelito got the shovel. Mamá got the watering can.

29   "Ready, Oscar?" asked Papá.

30   "I'm ready!" Oscar looked around at his family and grinned. "We'll have a beautiful tree right in front of our house for all of us to enjoy.

31   Papá dug a hole. Oscar held the tree in place as Magdalena, Abuelita, and Abuelito gently pushed dirt around it. When they were finished, Mamá sprinkled water on top.

32   Everyone stood back to admire the new tree. Oscar couldn't wait to watch it grow.

GO ON

© Houghton Mifflin Harcourt Publishing Company. All rights reserved.

Name _____ Date _____

18 Which word has about the same meaning as <u>bounded</u> in paragraph 1?

   F Hid

   G Strolled

   H Bounced

   J Trembled

19 Oscar's problem with his tree is that he—

   A thinks it is too small to survive

   B cannot read the directions for planting

   C is unsure where to plant it

   D fears his family will not want it

20 What happens before Oscar hears his family's stories about their special trees?

   F He gets his own tree from school.

   G He plants his tree with his family.

   H He decides where to plant his tree.

   J He reads the directions for planting.

21 Because of the tree in her yard, Mamá had—

   A enjoyed agua de limón

   B learned how to be alone and rest

   C met her best friend

   D spent a lot of time with her father

22 How is the tree that Papá describes different from the ones Oscar's other family members describe?

   F Papá's tree produces fruit, but the others' trees do not.

   G Papá's tree does not live long, but the others' trees are fully grown.

   H Papá's tree grows in their backyard, but the others' trees grow in other places.

   J Papá's tree is enjoyed just by him, but the others' trees are enjoyed by many.

23 Oscar plants his tree—

   A next to the sidewalk

   B on the other side of town

   C in their backyard

   D at the edge of a cornfield

GO ON

© Houghton Mifflin Harcourt Publishing Company. All rights reserved.

> Read this selection. Then answer the questions that follow it.
> Mark your answer on the Answer Document.

Ben Liang's Story

1   Ben Liang slumped over at his desk in school and stared dejectedly at a blank piece of paper in front of him, worrying about his latest homework assignment. His teacher, Ms. Valdez, had just said to the class, "For the past couple of weeks, we have been reading stories about family, adventures, and pets. Today I want each of you to compose a story about your family, an adventure, or a pet." Ben's spirits plummeted. He had no idea what to write about, and he contemplated his story's topic as he gazed at the sheet of white paper.

2   Ben and his family had immigrated to America from China when he was still a toddler. His father and mother purchased a small Chinese restaurant, and the apartment upstairs became home to Ben, his father and mother, his grandmother, and his younger sister, Emily. Before he began attending his new school, Ben enjoyed helping his mother and grandmother fold dumplings for their customers. While they prepared the food, they would practice speaking English together. Ben thought that this cherished time with his family might make a good story.

3   Or Ben could write about feasting on *dim sum*, his favorite Chinese meal, every week with his family and friends. In Chinese, *dim sum* means "a little bit of the heart." Ben thought that was an excellent name because the variety of foods on the *dim sum* table (Chinese dumplings, extraordinary meat dishes, and lots of fresh, hot vegetables) is made from the heart.

4   On *dim sum* days, Ben and his cousins scampered and played among the empty tables in his parents' restaurant before the customers arrived. One morning, the children quietly opened the kitchen door to watch the cooks making *dim sum*. Suddenly one cook collided with a cart full of food, everything went crashing to the floor, and everyone went running to the kitchen to help. Ben and his relatives labored hard all that day to make more food. Ben smiled as he recalled the *dim sum* incident and thought that perhaps Ms. Valdez would enjoy reading that story.

© Houghton Mifflin Harcourt Publishing Company. All rights reserved.

Name _____ Date _____

5   Then Ben remembered one special Sunday when his father took him along with his mother, sister, and grandmother to a nearby park for a day of relaxation. In the center of the park was a big lake surrounded by tall, green pine trees. Ben's father rented a rowboat and took Ben and Emily out on the lake.

6   Ben heard his mother shout, "Look, turtles!" She pointed, and Ben's father started rowing in that direction. There, near the bank of the lake, they spotted, dozens of turtles.

7   "Let's catch one," Ben's father suggested, and Ben and Emily nodded eagerly. As Ben's father rowed nearer to the swimming creatures, Ben reached over the side of the boat to seize one of the biggest turtles.

8   "I got it!" he yelled as he scooped the turtle into the boat.

9   "He's huge," giggled Emily. She turned to her father and asked, "Can we keep him?"

10   Ben's father laughed. "Sure we can," he said. "We can put him in the wading pool I bought for you and Ben a couple of years ago. You will have to be responsible, take very good care of him, and think of a name for him."

11   What an adventure that had been! Ben smiled to himself, thinking that he still had that turtle, and it was the greatest pet he'd ever owned. He had named his turtle Dim Sum because he thought his pet was a "bit of the heart," just like his favorite family meal.

12   Ben eventually began to relax as he started writing his assignment for Ms. Valdez. The title of his story would be "Dim Sum: My Pet Turtle."

© Houghton Mifflin Harcourt Publishing Company. All rights reserved.

Name _____ Date _____

24 Ben is unhappy at the beginning of the story because—

    F he does not like sitting at his desk

    G his teacher is boring him

    H he does not know what to write about

    J his father purchases a Chinese restaurant

25 Going to the lake is important to the story because—

    A the lake is full of turtles

    B it is a special Sunday for Ben's family

    C Ben gets an idea for his story at the lake

    D the family eats *dim sum* at the lake

26 Which sentence from the story states a fact?

    F *In Chinese,* dim sum *means 'a little bit of the heart.'*

    G *Ben thought that was an excellent name because the variety of foods on the* dim sum *table is made from the heart.*

    H *"He's huge," giggled Emily.*

    J *Ben smiled to himself, thinking that he still had that turtle, and it was the greatest pet he'd ever owned.*

27 How will Ben most likely feel when he is finished with his story?

    A Strange

    B Proud

    C Comical

    D Ordinary

> **Read this selection. Then read answer the questions that follow it.
> Mark your answer on the Answer Document.**

All About Robots

1   Did you know that you have robots in your home? Every time an alarm clock rings, you are hearing a robot. When your mother puts food in the microwave, she is using a robot. When you put a movie in to watch, you are using a robot. Robots have many uses.

2   What is a robot? A robot is a machine that can do work that is normally done by people. The robot is run by a computer, which acts as its "brain." The <u>brain</u> tells the robot what to do.

3   Robots do many jobs that people do not want to do. They build cars, make parts for machines, and even make candy bars. Many companies use robots because they never get sick, they do not need to eat, and they never have to rest.

4   Some robots do jobs that are not safe for people to do. For example, the planet Mars would be a dangerous place to visit. So scientists sent robots, instead of people, to check out Mars. The robots gathered important information about Mars. They then relayed that information back to Earth. This helps everyone to know more about the red planet.

5   Robots can go other places that would not be safe for people. They can go into burning buildings and help put out fires. Scientists use robots to go inside volcanoes and study what is happening. Robots can also be used to learn about the ocean, because they can dive far deeper than people. They gather information about fish and plants that people have never seen before.

© Houghton Mifflin Harcourt Publishing Company. All rights reserved.

6   Soon robots may be used for even more important jobs. They could help police, doctors, farmers, and families. Yes, there may be even more robots in your home. Robots to help you clean the house and even to make you lemonade!

7   Look at the chart to learn about some of the early advances in robot history.

Early Advances in Robotics

Year	Inventor	Nationality	Invention(s)
350 B.C.	Archytas	Greek	Mechanical bird
About 200 B.C.	Ctesibus	Greek	Water clocks
1495	Leonardo DaVinci	Italian	Knight in armor
1738	Jacques de Vaucanson	French	Two musical players and a duck
1770	Pierre and Henri-Louis Jaquet-Droz	Swiss	Three dolls

GO ON

© Houghton Mifflin Harcourt Publishing Company. All rights reserved.

Name _____ Date _____

28 What does the author use to introduce the definition of "robot"?

F A question

G An exclamation

H Underlining

J Italics

29 In paragraph 2, what does the word <u>brain</u> mean?

A The front part of the head

B A person who is very intelligent

C The device to control functions

D A person who is a good planner

30 According to information in the article, what is most likely true about the future of robots?

F Inventors will learn from their mistakes.

G Inventors will continue to make better robots.

H Inventors will start learning more from the past.

J Inventors will stop sending robots to places that are unsafe.

31 Which column of the chart would the reader use to find out which inventor was Italian?

A Year

B Inventor

C Nationality

D Invention(s)

32 According to the chart, Archytas and Ctesibus are alike because both—

F made inventions in the same year

G have the same last name

H invented something musical

J shared the same nationality

BE SURE TO MARK YOUR ANSWERS ON THE ANSWER DOCUMENT. | STOP |

Writing: Revising and Editing

Read the introduction and the passage that follows it. Then read each question. Mark your answers on the Answer Document.

Elise is in fourth grade. She wrote this story about life on a farm. She wants you to help her revise and edit the story. Read Elise's story and think about the changes she should make. Then answer the questions that follow.

A Day on the Farm

(1) On a typical morning, you probably wake up, get dressed, and go to school. (2) I do all these things too, and more. (3) During the week my sister and I wake up before the sun rises and start working immediately. (4) That's because my family lives on a farm. (5) It has been in our family since the civil war.

(6) First, we feed our pet, Max the dog and Henry the cat. (7) Then we put on boots and walk to the barn. (8) Most mornings we have to use a flashlight to find our way. (9) We feed both the chickens but the dairy cows. (10) It is important to make sure all of the animals have plenty of water and clean stalls. (11) Our last chore is to gather the eggs from the chicken coop for breakfast. (12) Yesterday we taked 12 fresh eggs back to the house.

GO ON

(13) After we've finished our morning chores, we eat breakfast with Mom and Dad. (14) Then we put on our backpacks and walk to the bus stop.

(15) While we are at school, Mom and Dad completes the remainder of the chores. (16) They take care of the fields where we grow corn and beans. (17) When my sister and I arrive home from school, we do our homework and eat a healthful snack. (18) Then we have time to play.

(19) Afterward, we eat dinner together, and we always go to bed early.

(20) Our life on the farm may be busier than most people's, but we keep usselves entertained!

---

1 What change, if any, should be made in sentence 5?

   A Change *has been* to **have being**

   B Insert a comma after *family*

   C Change *civil war* to **Civil War**

   D Make no change

2 What change should be made in sentence 6?

   F Change *pet* to **pets**

   G Delete the comma after *pet*

   H Change *Max* to **max**

   J Change *cat* to **Cat**

© Houghton Mifflin Harcourt Publishing Company. All rights reserved.

Name _____ Date _____

3 What change should be made in sentence 9?

   A Change *feed* to **fed**

   B Insert a comma after *chickens*

   C Change *but* to **and**

   D Change *dairy* to **Dairy**

4 What change should be made in sentence 12?

   F Insert **have** after *we*

   G Change *taked* to **took**

   H Change *fresh* to **freshest**

   J Insert a comma after **eggs**

5 Which sentence could **BEST** follow and support sentence 14?

   A I got a new backpack last week because my old one wore out.

   B One of our cows has a new calf, and it needs a lot of attention.

   C My mother and father went to my school when they were children.

   D The school bus picks us up, and we arrive at school just before the bell rings.

6 What change, if any, should be made in sentence 15?

   F Change *we* to **they**

   G Delete the comma after *school*

   H Change *completes* to **complete**

   J Make no change

7 What change should be made in sentence 20?

   A Insert a comma after *farm*

   B Change *busier* to **busyer**

   C Delete the comma after **people's**

   D Change *usselves* to **ourselves**

GO ON

© Houghton Mifflin Harcourt Publishing Company. All rights reserved.

> **Read the introduction and the passage that follows it. Then read each question. Mark your answers on the Answer Document.**

Sam wrote this report about bats. He would like you to read his paper and think about the corrections and improvements he needs to make. When you finish reading, answer the questions that follow.

Bats

(1) Some peoples think that bats are scary, but they are actually interesting, helpful animals. (2) Bats are mammals. (3) In fact, they are the only mammals that can truly fly. (4) This is just one interesting fact about bats. (5) The more you know about bats the more you realize how fascinating they is.

(6) Insects are the ones who should be afraid of bats. (7) Some bats can eat their own wait in insects in one night. (8) That's a skill you might be thankful for if you've ever had an itchy mosquito bite. (9) Poison ivy can also make you itch.

(10) Some bats fertilize plants as they fly from one plant to another, feeding on the nectar and pollen of flowers. (11) Bats scatter plant seeds as they fly, too. (12) Both of these actions. (13) Help new plants to grow.

(14) When it comes to finding their way around, bats an unusual set of skills. (15) Many types of bats do not see well, so they use their hearing in a very special way to help them "see" things. (16) Bats make high pitched sounds and listen to the echoes as the sounds bounce off of objects. (17) Bats use this unusual method of seeing as they go very, very fast though the air and hunt at night.

GO ON

8 What change should be made in sentence 1?

   F Change *peoples* to **people**

   G Delete the comma after *scary*

   H Change *but* to **and**

   J Change *interesting* to **interest**

9 What change should be made in sentence 5?

   A Change *know* to **knew**

   B Insert a period after *bats*

   C Change *fascinating* to **fascinated**

   D Change *is* to **are**

10 What change should be made in sentence 7?

   F Change *eat* to **eating**

   G Change *their* to **they're**

   H Change *wait* to **weight**

   J Change *insects* to **insectes**

11 What revision, if any, is needed in sentences 12 and 13?

   A Both of these actions help new plants to grow.

   B Both of these. Actions help new plants to grow.

   C Both of these actions and they help new plants to grow.

   D No revision is needed.

12 What change should be made in sentence 14?

   F Change *finding* to **find**

   G Insert **have** after *bats*

   H Change *set* to **sit**

   J Change *skills* to **skill**

13 What change is needed in sentence 17?

   A Change *use* to **used**

   B Change *unusual* to **unusually**

   C Insert a period after *seeing*

   D Change *go very, very fast* to **speed**

14 Which sentence does **NOT** belong in the report?

   F Sentence 3

   G Sentence 9

   H Sentence 11

   J Sentence 16

© Houghton Mifflin Harcourt Publishing Company. All rights reserved.

Read the introduction and the passage that follows it. Then read each question. Mark your answers on the Answer Document.

Darcy wrote a story about her grandparents. She wants you to help her revise and edit it. Read Darcy's story and think about the changes you would make. Then answer the questions that follow.

My Family

(1) If you could go anywhere in the worlds, where would you go? (2) I would go either to Italy and Japan. (3) That is because my grandmother is from Japan and my grandfather is from Italy. (4) They meeted in the United States more than 50 years ago.

(5) I love visiting my grandparents. (6) Seeing them always rominds me of our unique heritage. (7) My grandmother likes to make many of the dish she ate as a child in Japan. (8) My favorite food she makes is called katsudon, a dish that has rice, egg, and meat.

(9) I always see my grandmother on May 5. (10) On that day, we celebrate a japanese holiday called Children's Day, to recognize the happiness of children. (11) My grandmother hangs a brightly colored kite in the shape of a fish outside my door.

© Houghton Mifflin Harcourt Publishing Company. All rights reserved.

(12) My grandfather enjoy sharing his heritage with me, too. (13) Every time we see him, he kisses each family member twice, once on each cheek.

(14) Like my grandmother, he enjoys cooking foods from his childhood.

(15) He has taught me how to make pasta.

15 What change, if any, should be made in sentence 1?

  A Change *in* to **of**

  B Change *worlds* to **world**

  C Change the question mark to a period

  D Make no change

16 What change should be made in sentence 2?

  F Change *would* to **will**

  G Change *either* to **neither**

  H Change *Italy* to **italy**

  J Change *and* to **or**

17 What change should be made in sentence 4?

  A Change *meeted* to **met**

  B Change *United States* to **united states**

  C Change *than* to **then**

  D Change *years* to **year**

18 What change should be made in sentence 7?

  F Change *make* to **makes**

  G Insert a comma after *many*

  H Change *dish* to **dishes**

  J Change *a* to **the**

GO ON

© Houghton Mifflin Harcourt Publishing Company. All rights reserved.

19 What change, if any, should be made in sentence 10?

   A Delete the comma after *day*

   B Change *japanese* to **Japanese**

   C Change *Children's* to **children's**

   D Make no change

20 Which sentence could **BEST** follow and support sentence 11?

   F Once I entered a kite-flying contest.

   G My favorite holiday is Thanksgiving.

   H My grandmother is a really good cook.

   J The fish represents courage and strength.

21 What change should be made in sentence 12?

   A Change *grandfather* to **Grandfather**

   B Change *enjoy* to **enjoys**

   C Change *sharing* to **share**

   D Change *his* to **he's**

BE SURE TO MARK YOUR ANSWERS ON THE ANSWER DOCUMENT.

STOP

Name _____ Date _____

Writing: Written Composition

> Write a composition to persuade the reader
> that your town is a great place to live.

Use a separate sheet of paper to plan your composition. Then write your composition on the lined pages that follow.

The information in the box below will help you remember what you should think about when you write your persuasive essay.

REMEMBER—YOU SHOULD

❏ write to persuade the reader that your town is a great place to live

❏ state your opinion clearly

❏ support your opinion with clearly-stated reasons, facts, and examples

❏ include an introduction, body, and conclusion

❏ try to use correct spelling, capitalization, punctuation, grammar, and sentences

---

Name _____ Date _____

_____

_____

_____

_____

_____

_____

_____

_____

_____

_____

_____

_____

_____

_____

© Houghton Mifflin Harcourt Publishing Company. All rights reserved.

Name _____ Date _____

_____

_____

_____

_____

_____

_____

_____

_____

_____

_____

_____

_____

_____

_____

_____

© Houghton Mifflin Harcourt Publishing Company. All rights reserved.

Reading

> **Read the next two selections. Then answer the questions that follow them. Mark your answers on the Answer Document.**

Help for Dogs

Joseph worked to raise money for an animal shelter. He wrote about his experience in a journal. Here is part of Joseph's journal.

1   **March 14**—Today a piece of mail caught my eye. My mom opened the envelope, glanced at the paper, and put it into the recycling bin. I saw pictures of dogs, so I pulled it out of the bin and read it. It was from a local animal shelter. The paper showed dogs that had been rescued and were in need of a good home. The letter that accompanied the pictures explained that the shelter was in need of money to pay for dog food, <u>medicine</u>, and other bills. I want to help the dogs at the shelter.

2   **March 15**—I showed the letter from the animal shelter to my friend Carlos. He said that he wanted to help, too. It gave me the idea of asking everyone in the neighborhood to help raise money for the shelter. My mother said I should come up with a plan and present it to Mrs. Young, the <u>head</u> of the local community center. I have an <u>appointment</u> to talk to Mrs. Young tomorrow.

3   **March 16**—I <u>proposed</u> my idea to Mrs. Young, and she loved it! We're going to have a family game night at the center. People will bring games to play with other families. We will charge five dollars per family to attend. We will sell snacks, too. Of course, people can <u>donate</u> more money if they would like. I have a lot of planning and organizing to do!

4   **April 2**—Family game night is tomorrow! Today after school I set up everything in the center's cafeteria. I hope that many families will come. I asked a newspaper reporter to come, too. People may have their picture in the paper. I hope that the <u>publicity</u> will inspire other people in the community to give a <u>donation</u> to the shelter.

5   **April 4**—Game night was extremely successful! Thirty-seven families came to play games. We raised almost $300 for the animal shelter. I'm very excited to give them the money.

The Hike

Tamara faced a challenge she did not think she could overcome. She wrote about her feelings in her journal. Here is part of Tamara's journal.

1   **February 4**—Everyone is excited about our field trip tomorrow. Everyone except for me, that is. We're going to a park where there is a climbing rock with trails that lead you from the ground to the <u>summit</u>. It is almost 500 feet high.

2   The climbing rock may as well be the gigantic Mount Everest! There is no way I'll reach the top of it. Though I'd like to be an athlete, I just don't seem to have the skills for most sports. My legs refuse to carry me very fast when I run. My absolute least favorite time of day is gym. When Coach Case begins to describe a game, I slowly try to make myself invisible so I don't have to play. Maybe I'll wake up sick and have to stay home tomorrow.

3   **February 5**—You will not believe what happened today! I actually made it to the summit all by myself! I believe it may have been the most rewarding experience of my life so far. Let me tell you all about it.

4   First, I woke up and tried to tell Mom I was too sick to go to school. She eyed me suspiciously as she took my temperature. Of course, it was normal, so she would not let me stay home. As soon as I arrived at school, the teacher checked to be sure we all had our hats, water bottles, and sunscreen. I got on the school bus with a heavy heart and took a seat next to my friend Anita. Soon we were at the park and getting off of the bus.

5   With water bottles in hand, we gathered at the bottom of the rock to start the hike. The guides made sure we were all wearing our safety helmets correctly. I decided to be like the tortoise instead of the <u>hare</u> and take a slow and steady pace. As I started the hike, I saw interesting rock formations and <u>unusual</u> reptiles. When I saw other kids stopping to catch their breath, I realized that I felt fine. In fact, I felt fantastic! I continued my slow, steady climb until I reached the top. I felt like I was on top of the world! I never wanted to come down.

6   After about 30 minutes, it was time to start our descent. I caught myself going down the trail with a spring in my step. My heart <u>swelled</u> with pride as I thought about what I'd accomplished. Watch out, Mount Everest, here I come!

GO ON ➡

Use "Help for Dogs" to answer questions 1–6.

1 What happens right after Joseph shows Carlos the letter from the shelter?

A Joseph gives money to the animal shelter.

B Joseph talks to Mrs. Young at the community center.

C Joseph thinks of asking neighbors to help the shelter.

D Joseph asks a reporter to come to the community center.

2 Which definition represents the meaning of <u>head</u> as it is used in paragraph 2?

> **head** /hed/ *noun* **1.** the part of the body containing the brain, eyes, ears, nose, and mouth **2.** mental ability **3.** the main side of a coin **4.** a person who leads or is in charge of something

F Definition 1

G Definition 2

H Definition 3

J Definition 4

3 What does the word <u>proposed</u> mean in paragraph 3?

A Asked for help

B Solved a problem

C Suggested a course of action

D Organized a community event

4 What happens on April 2?

F Joseph talks to Mrs. Young.

G Joseph prepares the community center.

H Families play games at the community center.

J A reporter writes an article about the animal shelter.

5 In paragraph 4, what does the word <u>publicity</u> mean?

A Something meant to get the public's attention

B Something done in public to benefit neighbors

C An event designed to raise money for a cause

D A desire to appear in a newspaper for others to see

6 What does the word <u>donation</u> mean in paragraph 4?

F News printed in an article

G Time spent helping others

H Money given to help others

J Pictures printed in a newspaper

GO ON

Use "The Hike" to answer questions 7–11.

---

7 Which words in paragraph 1 help the reader understand what <u>summit</u> means?

  A *field trip tomorrow*

  B *except for me*

  C *We're going to a park*

  D *from the ground to*

8 Why does Tamara want to miss the field trip?

  F She is too sick to go.

  G She is afraid of heights.

  H She has a hurt leg and cannot run.

  J She does not think she can reach the top.

9 What is the first thing that happens on February 5?

  A Tamara reaches the summit.

  B Tamara rides on the school bus.

  C Tamara tells her Mom she is sick.

  D Tamara puts on her safety helmet.

10 In paragraph 5, what does the word <u>hare</u> mean?

  F A person who is good at sports

  G Fine strands that grow on a person's head

  H An animal with fur, long ears, and long legs

  J A guide who leads groups of hikers on trails

11 In paragraph 6, the word <u>swelled</u> means—

  A felt afraid

  B became larger

  C jumped in fear

  D pounded heavily

GO ON

Use "Help for Dogs" and "The Hike" to answer questions 12–18.

12 How are Tamara and Joseph alike?

F They both defeat a fear.

G They both do something rewarding.

H They both do something to help others.

J They both think they will be unsuccessful.

13 One idea present in both of these selections is—

A winning contests

B meeting new people

C overcoming challenges

D raising money for a cause

14 How are Joseph's feelings before the game night different from Tamara's feelings before the hike?

F Joseph feels nervous. Tamara feels calm.

G Joseph feels relaxed. Tamara feels bored.

H Joseph feels excited. Tamara feels unhappy.

J Joseph feels uncertain. Tamara feels confident.

15 The word <u>donate</u> has the same sound for <u>t</u> as—

A waited

B capture

C motion

D latch

16 The word <u>medicine</u> has the same sound for <u>c</u> as—

F peaches

G jacket

H advice

J fabric

17 What does the word <u>appointment</u> mean?

A Job

B Game

C Meeting

D Practice

18 What does the word <u>unusual</u> mean?

F Not common

G Growing larger

H Does not exist

J Like something else

GO ON

© Houghton Mifflin Harcourt Publishing Company. All rights reserved.

Read this selection. Then answer the questions that follow it.
Mark your answers on the Answer Document.

Brookview Times

February 27   Volume 10, Issue 14

City Asks Children for Help
by Lisa Depont

1   The city of Brookview invites families who live in the city to attend a meeting with the Planning Board to talk about the City Development Project. The meeting will be held March 3, at 6:30 in the evening, at the Community Center.

2   Last year the board asked people to fill out a survey with questions about how it could improve the community. Next, the board made a plan based on the survey results. One part of the plan is to build a new park in downtown Brookview.

3   At the March 3 meeting, the board wants to hear from the children of Brookview. Children will have the opportunity to tell what they would like to see in the new park. The board will display pictures of parks in other cities. Children will be asked to study the pictures and note the features of the parks they like best, such as bike trails, playgrounds, and picnic tables. Children can also bring their own pictures to show what they would like in the park.

4   After the meeting, the board will use the children's feedback to make three plans for the new park. In May, there will be a second meeting where people can vote for the plan they like the best. Their votes will decide which park will be built. It will be a year before the new park is ready for use. The city is planning a ceremony in the new park next May.

5   The city will continue to hold meetings to foster community involvement and to tell people about the park and its progress. The next part of the plan is to resurface streets and add sidewalks and crosswalks around the park to make it easier for people to visit shops and restaurants downtown. This part should start next summer after the park is open.

GO ON

City Asks Children for Help *continued*

Kids, we want to hear your voices!

6   The new park you <u>deserve</u> is coming to Brookview! Help us design it. Do you want a place to in-line skate? Do you want a cool, new playground with a giant slide? The choice is yours! Come let your voice be heard and turn the park of your imagination into reality.

7   The city's Planning Board is holding a meeting on March 3 to <u>discuss</u> part one of the City Development Project. The board needs your ideas to help design the new park.

8   Brookview Town Hall Meeting
March 3 at 6:30 P.M.
Community Center, 702 Main Street

9   For more <u>information</u> on the City Development Project or the new park, call 555-1336 or visit the city's website.

GO ON

19 Which detail best supports the main idea that the city of Brookview values people's opinions?

A The city is planning a ceremony.

B The Planning Board is having a meeting on March 3.

C The city built a Community Center where people have meetings.

D The Planning Board asked people how it could improve the community.

20 Which words in paragraph 2 help the reader understand what survey means?

F *with questions about*

G *last year the board*

H *made a plan based*

J *to build a new park in*

21 In paragraph 2, the word downtown means—

A a large city

B two nearby towns

C the center of the city

D a playground in a park

22 At the March 3 meeting, children will be asked to—

F draw pictures of parks

G add sidewalks to a park

H vote on a plan for a park

J give their ideas for a park

23 What does the word second mean in paragraph 4?

A After the first

B Less important

C One-sixtieth of a minute

D A note in a musical scale

24 In paragraph 4, the word ceremony means—

F a task that must be done

G a place where people can gather

H an event to celebrate something

J a project to improve a community

25 What does the word foster mean in paragraph 5?

A Fight

B Accept

C Persuade

D Encourage

GO ON

© Houghton Mifflin Harcourt Publishing Company. All rights reserved.

26 Look at the chart below and use it to answer the question below.

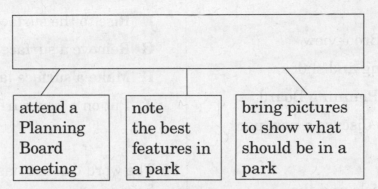

| attend a Planning Board meeting | note the best features in a park | bring pictures to show what should be in a park |

Which of the following belongs in the empty box?

F Brookview Has Planning Board Help Plan for City's Future

G Brookview Has Children Help Design New Community Park

H People in Brookview Have Power to Make Planning Board Do What They Want

J People in Brookview Tell Planning Board How to Improve Community

---

27 The word <u>deserve</u> in paragraph 6 means—

A ought to have

B have asked for

C would like to have

D have wanted for a long time

28 Paragraph 6 was written to persuade readers to—

F think of ideas for the new park

G use the new park for in-line skating

H come to the new park when it opens

J choose a giant slide for the new park

29 What does the word <u>information</u> mean in paragraph 9?

A Ideas

B Opinions

C Knowledge

D Permission

30 Which words from the advertisement are used to persuade?

F *let your voice be heard*

G *holding a meeting*

H *discuss part one*

J *visit the city's website*

GO ON

© Houghton Mifflin Harcourt Publishing Company. All rights reserved.

31 What is the advertisement mainly about?

   A Children in Brookview

   B In-line skating and slides

   C Brookview's Planning Board

   D A meeting to discuss a new park

32 How are the article and the advertisement alike?

   F Both tell readers to visit the city's website.

   G Both invite readers to come to the ceremony next May.

   H Both state that the Planning Board wants readers' opinions.

   J Both give facts about what the Planning Board did last year.

33 Which of these shows the correct way to divide the word community into syllables?

   A com • mu • ni • ty

   B co • mmun • i • ty

   C comm • u • nit • y

   D com • mun • it • y

34 What does the word resurface mean?

   F Rise to the surface

   G Remove a surface

   H Make a surface larger

   J Put on a new surface

35 The word discuss has the same sound for underline(s) as—

   A vision

   B sure

   C similar

   D mission

BE SURE TO MARK YOUR ANSWERS ON THE ANSWER DOCUMENT.

STOP

Writing: Revising and Editing

> **Read the introduction and the passage that follows it. Then read each question. Mark your answers on the Answer Document.**

Myra wrote this narrative about a vacation she took last summer. She wants you to help her correct it. Read Myra's narrative and think about the changes she should make. Then answer the questions that follow.

Summer Vacation

(1) Last summer, my dad decided that we should take an unusual vacation. (2) I said I wanted to go to the beach, but Dad insisted on something else. (3) He gave each of us an assignment. (4) My brothers and I had to find a roadside attraction that we thought the family would enjoy.

(5) It could not be farther than 200 miles away from our home, and we could not share our location with each other.

(6) About a week before our trip, each of us met secret with Dad.

(7) We gave him information around our chosen location. (8) Then he

plotted our route on a map.

(9) It was time for our trip. (10) We were all excited about the

uncertainty of the trip. (11) Where would we go? (12) What would we see?

(13) Our first stop was Austin's Cathedral of Junk. (14) My older

brother, Erik, Jr, found this one. (15) Dad said he probably chose the

location because it reminded him of his intidy room. (16) Then we drove

south to Poteet where we saw the world's largest strawberry. (17) It was

made of metal, of course. (18) The next stop was a huge ice cream cone

in Port Isabel. (19) It was an ice cream shop in the shape of an ice cream

cone. (20) Dad surprised us with the last one. (21) It was a store on South

Padre Island. (22) The entrance was a huge shark with an open mouth.

(23) When we left the store, we went to the beach. (24) It was a vacation!

GO ON

© Houghton Mifflin Harcourt Publishing Company. All rights reserved.

1 Which sentence could **BEST** be added after sentence 2?

   A Everyone in my family likes to eat ice cream.

   B We live in a small town outside Austin, Texas.

   C Some people enjoy going to the beach for vacation.

   D We would drive around Texas to see roadside attractions.

2 What change, if any, should be made in sentence 6?

   F Change *About* to **Into**

   G Delete the comma after *trip*

   H Change *secret* to **secretly**

   J Make no change

3 What change, if any, should be made in sentence 7?

   A Change *We* to **They**

   B Change *around* to **about**

   C Change *chosen* to **chose**

   D Make no change

4 Which transition word or phrase could **BEST** be added to the beginning of sentence 9?

   F First,

   G Finally,

   H As a result,

   J In conclusion,

5 What change should be made in sentence 14?

   A Change *My* to **The**

   B Insert a comma after *older*

   C Insert a period after *Jr*

   D Change *this* to **that**

6 What change should be made in sentence 15?

   F Change *chose* to **choosed**

   G Change *because* to **until**

   H Change *him* to **he**

   J Change *intidy* to **untidy**

7 What change, if any, should be made in sentence 24?

   A Change *was* to **were**

   B Insert **great** before *vacation*

   C Change the exclamation mark to a question mark

   D Make no change

> **Read each introduction and the passage that follows it. Then read each question. Mark your answers on the Answer Document.**

Manuel wrote this paper about something exciting that happened to him. Read Manuel's paper and think about the changes he should make. Then answer the questions that follow.

The Winning Poem

(1) Have you ever entered a contest? (2) I've entered alot of them, but I never win. (3) At least I never won until now. (4) Recently my friend, Julia, told me about a poetry-writing contest. (5) I love to write poetry, so I thought it would be a very, very nice contest for me.

(6) Mom and I used the Internet to read the rules on the contest's website. (7) Then I wrote the perfect poem. (8) I wrote a poem about writing poetry. (9) The poem is about how difficult it is to find just the right words and how wonderful it is to be able to express yourself through words in a poem. (10) I e-mailed the poem in the address on the Internet and tried to forget about the contest.

(11) After six long weeks, I received a reply. (12) I was so excited to read the letter, which began with the wonderful words, "Dear Mr Shaw, Congratulations!" (13) The envelope had a check for my winning poem, but the best part of all was seeing my poem in print in the magazine for everyone to read!

GO ON ➡

© Houghton Mifflin Harcourt Publishing Company. All rights reserved.

8 What change should be made in sentence 2?

   F Change *alot* to **a lot**

   G Delete the comma after **them**

   H Change *I* to **you**

   J Change *win* to **wins**

9 What change should be made in sentence 5?

   A Change *write* to **make**

   B Insert a comma after *thought*

   C Change *a very, very nice* to **the perfect**

   D Change *me* to **I**

10 Which transition word or phrase could **BEST** be added to the beginning of sentence 6?

   F First,

   G At last,

   H In fact,

   J In addition,

11 Which sentence should be added after sentence 6?

   A Mom uses the computer for work sometimes.

   B This was the first writing contest I ever entered.

   C Julia was certain I had a good chance of winning.

   D When we were done, I wrote down ideas for a poem.

12 What change should be made in sentence 10?

   F Change *in* to **to**

   G Change *and* to **next**

   H Change *tried* to **try**

   J Change *forget* to **forgot**

13 Which transition word or phrase could **BEST** be added to the beginning of sentence 11?

   A Now,

   B Next,

   C Finally,

   D In addition,

14 What change should be made in sentence 12?

   F Change *excited* to **happy**

   G Change *which* to **and**

   H Insert a comma after *Dear*

   J Insert a period after *Mr*

GO ON

© Houghton Mifflin Harcourt Publishing Company. All rights reserved.

> **Read the introduction and the passage that follows it. Then read each question. Mark your answers on the Answer Document.**

Amelia's fourth grade class read about rainbows. She wrote this report to tell about her findings. She wants you to read her paper and help correct her errors.

Rainbows

(1) The light we usually see is called visible light. (2) Although this light may appear colorless or white, it is actually made up of differently colors, which are also called a spectrum. (3) In a spectrum, colors always appear in a specific order: red, orange, yellow, green, blue, indigo, and violet. (4) The easiest way to remember the colors of the visible spectrum is to remember the name Roy G Biv. (5) Each letter stands for a color—R is for red, O is for orange, Y is for yellow, G is for green, B is for blue, I is for indigo, and V is for violet. (6) These are the colors of a rainbow.

(7) Do you know what makes a rainbow? (8) Light passes through water, such as drops of rain, or a piece of glass. (9) The light bends or splits, allowing you to see the different colors. (10) You normal see a rainbow when it is raining and the sun is shining at the same time.

(11) The sun will be behind you and the rainbow in front to you.

(12) Now when you see a beautifull rainbow, you'll understand why it appears.

---

15 What change should be made in sentence 2?

  A Change *Although* to **But**

  B Change *made* to **make**

  C Change *differently* to **different**

  D Change *called* to **calls**

16 What change should be made in sentence 4?

  F Change *easiest* to **most easy**

  G Change *colors* to **colored**

  H Insert a comma after *is*

  J Insert a period after *G*

17 What change should be made in sentence 8?

  A Change *passes* to **pass**

  B Change *such as* to **example**

  C Change *drops of rain* to **raindrops**

  D Change *of* to **for**

18 Which transition word or phrase could **BEST** be added to the beginning of sentence 9?

  F First,

  G After,

  H As a result,

  J In conclusion,

© Houghton Mifflin Harcourt Publishing Company. All rights reserved.

19 What change should be made in sentence 10?

   A Change *normal* to **normally**

   B Change *is raining* to **are raining**

   C Change *shining* to **shone**

   D Change the period to a question mark

20 What change, if any, should be made in sentence 11?

   F Change *sun* to **sun's**

   G Change *be* to **been**

   H Change *to* to **of**

   J Make no change

21 What change, if any, should be made in sentence 12?

   A Change *see* to **sees**

   B Change *beautifull* to **beautiful**

   C Change *you'll* to **youl'l**

   D Make no change

BE SURE TO MARK YOUR ANSWERS ON THE ANSWER DOCUMENT.

(STOP)

© Houghton Mifflin Harcourt Publishing Company. All rights reserved.

Writing: Written Composition

Write a personal narrative about a time when you helped someone.

Use a separate sheet of paper to plan your composition. Then write your composition on the lined pages that follow.

The information in the box below will help you remember what you should think about when you write your composition.

REMEMBER—YOU SHOULD

❑ write about a time when you helped someone

❑ organize events in the order in which they happened

❑ include details to make your narrative interesting

❑ show your personal feelings about the events in your narrative

❑ try to use correct spelling, capitalization, punctuation, grammar, and sentences

© Houghton Mifflin Harcourt Publishing Company. All rights reserved.

_____

_____

_____

_____

_____

_____

_____

_____

_____

_____

_____

_____

_____

_____

_____

_____

_____

© Houghton Mifflin Harcourt Publishing Company. All rights reserved.

_____

_____

_____

_____

_____

_____

_____

_____

_____

_____

_____

_____

_____

_____

Reading

> **Read this selection. Then answer the questions that follow it.**
> **Mark your answer on the Answer Document.**

Lost Pet

1   "Ziggy!" Jasmine stood on the porch and called her cat, but no orange-and-white tabby strolled out from behind the shrubs, or from under the minivan in the driveway.

2   Jasmine checked under her bed and under her computer table.

3   "Ziggy, where are you hiding?"

4   Searching inside the house had proved fruitless, so Jasmine returned to the yard, calling and calling her cat as she combed every hiding place she could remember. Ziggy had never been missing for so long before. Worried, Jasmine decided to ask her parents for help.

5   She found her mother in the den. "Mom, have you seen Ziggy?" she asked.

6   "Not since early this morning," her mother replied.

7   Next, Jasmine asked her father the same question.

8   "I saw Ziggy strolling through the flowerbed, but that was hours ago," he said.

9   By now, Jasmine was sure Ziggy had gotten lost. It was time to take action, so she took a sheet of paper, sketched a picture of Ziggy, and then wrote "Lost Cat" and her phone number below the drawing. She included a detailed description of her cat: large orange tabby, golden eyes, and fluffy coat of fur. Jasmine photocopied the posters and asked her mother to help her hang them up around the neighborhood. Then they went home to wait for a call.

10   Within two hours, she received a phone call in answer to her ad. A friendly voice on the other line said, "My name is Mrs. Garcia, and I believe I have Ziggy."

© Houghton Mifflin Harcourt Publishing Company. All rights reserved.
107

11   Jasmine was so excited that she jumped up and down. Then she remembered to ask Mrs. Garcia for her address and phone number. Finally, she asked what had happened.

12   "A huge orange tabby just strolled into my yard this afternoon. He has been resting on the porch, and he looks very comfortable," she added.

13   "I'll be right over to see if it's Ziggy," Jasmine exclaimed. She and her parents climbed into their minivan and drove to Mrs. Garcia's house.

14   Once Jasmine and her parents got to Mrs. Garcia's house, they discovered that the tabby was indeed Jasmine's lost Ziggy. Jasmine immediately scooped him up in her arms, nuzzled him, and buried her face in the soft fur of his neck. Ziggy closed his eyes and purred, as if his wandering away and being found again had been the most natural thing in the world.

15   Jasmine slipped the cat into his carrier, snapped the latch shut, and slid the carrier into the minivan. Her parents thanked Mrs. Garcia for her help, and drove their daughter and her <u>beloved</u> pet back home.

16   The next afternoon, Jasmine spotted Mrs. Garcia walking down the street. Mrs. Garcia wore a worried expression on her face.

17   Jasmine waved to her and walked over. "Is something wrong?" she asked.

GO ON

© Houghton Mifflin Harcourt Publishing Company. All rights reserved.

18   "Yes, Jasmine. It's odd, coming so soon after your adventure with Ziggy, but today my dog, Diego, is missing."

19   "Tell me about him," Jasmine asked. Mrs. Garcia described Diego's looks and personality.

20   "Is he a beagle?" Jasmine asked, and Mrs. Garcia nodded yes.

21   "I can help," Jasmine said. "I'll make posters for you and put them up."

22   Jasmine went home and hurriedly sketched a picture of a beagle. She added Mrs. Garcia's phone number, Diego's name and description, and some details about how he got lost. Again she made photocopies, and again her mother helped her hang them up.

23   That evening, Mrs. Garcia called Jasmine with the happy report that someone had identified a lost beagle in his neighborhood as Diego.

24   "You used your experience with Ziggy to help me," said Mrs. Garcia. "I really appreciate it. I'd like to invite you and your parents over tomorrow to meet Diego and to have some cookies," she continued.

25   "I look forward to it," Jasmine replied. "I'm so happy that both of our stories had happy endings!"

1 Jasmine and Mrs. Garcia both—

   A have very large pets

   B know how to draw animals

   C lose their pets for a short time

   D have a cat and a dog in their homes

2 Jasmine draws a picture of Ziggy—

   F to show how much she loves her cat

   G to help people recognize Ziggy if they find him

   H to encourage the neighbors to have cats as pets

   J to give to her neighbor Mrs. Garcia

3 What happens before Jasmine offers to help Mrs. Garcia?

   A Jasmine asks if Mrs. Garcia's dog is a beagle.

   B Jasmine sketches pictures of a beagle.

   C Mrs. Garcia reports that someone found a lost beagle.

   D Mrs. Garcia invites Jasmine to have some cookies.

4 Mrs. Garcia finds Ziggy—

   F on her porch

   G in her garden

   H on the sidewalk

   J in her neighborhood

5 In paragraph 15, what does the word beloved mean?

   A Tired

   B Playful

   C Treasured

   D Mischievous

6 What will Mrs. Garcia most likely do if Diego gets lost again?

   F Wait for him to come home

   G Call Jasmine to help her

   H Check in her flowerbed

   J Call the local pet shelter

GO ON

© Houghton Mifflin Harcourt Publishing Company. All rights reserved.

Name _____ Date _____

**Read this selection. Then answer the questions that follow it.
Mark your answer on the Answer Document.**

Recycling

1   Have you ever used an old bag or box? If so, you have recycled. One way to recycle is to reuse old things in new ways. For example, you can make a desk organizer out of an egg carton, use the Sunday comics to wrap a present, or jot notes on the back of an old envelope.

2   Many cities recycle. Residents put the trash that can be recycled into special bins. Glass, plastic, newspaper, some metals, and sometimes foam are among the materials that are recycled. The bins are put out with the trash, and picked up by sanitation workers. They are then sorted and taken to processing plants and factories to make new products. Therefore, recycling means less garbage.

3   What becomes of our recycled objects? Many new products are made from old ones. For example, old foam is shredded and pressed together into a jumble of many-colored foam, which is stuffed into pillows or used as carpet padding. Old paper turns up on store shelves as paper towels, cardboard, pet beds, and even as copier paper. Glass bottles and jars may be crushed into tiny pieces and used to pave roads, or they may be ground up into sand-size particles that are used on golf courses.

4   Recycled plastic has many uses. It is used to make toys, pens, pencils, fences, flowerpots, and outdoor furniture. Some kinds of plastic are even used to make soft, warm clothes!

5   It is important to recycle. It helps us to have less garbage. It also keeps us from wasting the Earth's trees and metals. When we recycle, we are being smart and taking care of the Earth, ourselves, and our future.

© Houghton Mifflin Harcourt Publishing Company. All rights reserved.

6   Look at the graph to see how many tons of paper each city recycles in a year.

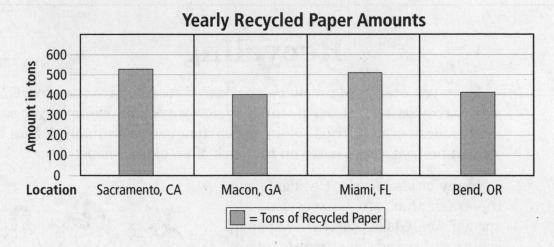

Yearly Recycled Paper Amounts

= Tons of Recycled Paper

7   Which reason best tells why the author wrote this article?

A   To inform readers about the benefits of recycling

B   To let readers know how to find a recycling center

C   To tell an entertaining story about recycling in one city

D   To convince readers to buy products made from garbage

8   According to the article, people at home can help reduce garbage by—

F   throwing out materials

G   grinding up glass

H   reusing materials

J   crushing up jars

9   According to the article, what will be the main problem if people choose not to recycle?

A   The earth's trees and metals will be wasted.

B   No new products will be developed.

C   Cities will have to hire more sanitation workers.

D   Cities will have to distribute more recycle bins.

10   In paragraph 3, what does the word jumble mean?

F   Pattern

G   Mixture

H   Picture

J   Order

GO ON

11 Which of the following sentences from the article states an opinion?

   A *One way to recycle is to use old things in new ways.*

   B *Residents put the trash that can be recycled into special bins.*

   C *Some kinds of plastic are even used to make soft, warm clothes!*

   D *It is important to recycle.*

12 According to the graph, the city that recycled the most paper was—

   F Bend, OR

   G Macon, GA

   H Miami, FL

   J Sacramento, CA

13 According to the graph, the city that recycled 400 tons of paper was—

   A Bend, OR

   B Macon, GA

   C Miami, FL

   D Sacramento, CA

> **Read this selection. Then answer the questions that follow it.**
> **Mark your answer on the Answer Document.**

The Library

by Barbara A. Huff

1 It looks like any building
When you pass it on the street,
Made of stone and glass and marble,
Made of iron and concrete.

2 But once inside you can ride
A camel or a train,
Visit Rome, Siam, or Nome,
Feel a hurricane,
Meet a king, learn to sing,
How to bake a pie,
Go to sea, plant a tree,
Find how airplanes fly,
Train a horse, and of course
Have all the dogs you'd like,
See the moon, a sandy dune,
Or catch a <u>whopping</u> pike.
Everything that books can bring
You'll find inside those walls.
A world is there for you to share
When adventure calls.

3 You cannot tell its magic
By the way the building looks,
But there's wonderment within it,
The wonderment of books.

© Houghton Mifflin Harcourt Publishing Company. All rights reserved.

14 What is the author referring to in the first two lines of the second stanza?

F Books about camels or trains

G Buying a train ticket

H Petting a camel

J Libraries near train tracks

15 The author compares the library to—

A other buildings

B people

C cities

D storms

16 In stanza 2, what does the word whopping mean?

F Travels

G Very busy

H In the desert

J Very large

17 Based on the poem, the reader can tell the author likes to—

A read

B eat

C write

D cook

Read this selection. Then answer the questions that follow it.
Mark your answer on the Answer Document.

Making a Journal

1   Mrs. Clark's students are making journals about their state. Each student will write five amazing facts about where they live and draw pictures about their state. Read Mrs. Clark's directions for making the journal.

Supplies:
- 10 pieces of <u>unlined</u> white paper
- 2 pieces of colored paper
- Crayons and markers

Directions:
On a piece of colored paper, complete the following tasks
- Write the title of your journal at the top of the page.
- Write your name at the bottom of the page.
- Draw a picture of your state.
- Place this page on top of the 10 pieces of white paper.
- Place the other piece of colored paper beneath the white papers.

2   After each student organizes his or her journal, Mrs. Clark punches holes in the journal pages so that each student can put the pages in order into a small binder. Then Mrs. Clark writes on the chalkboard what students should put in the journal.

Journal Information:
- On one journal page, write an amazing fact about your state.
- On the page next to it, draw a picture to <u>illustrate</u> that fact.
- You should have 5 amazing facts.

Parents' Night

3   When all students have completed their journals, Mrs. Clark will put the journals on display on special tables for visitors to see on Parents' Night.

Name _____ Date _____

18 What does the prefix *un-* suggest that the word <u>unlined</u> means in the list of supplies?

   F Below the lines

   G Having many lines

   H Between the lines

   J Not having lines

19 Which section tells the reader what is needed to make the journal?

   A Supplies

   B Directions

   C Journal Information

   D Parents' Night

20 Why does Mrs. Clark most likely write "Journal Information" on the chalkboard?

   F So she will remember what goes in the journals

   G So students know what to put in their journals

   H So students know what to bring for Parents' Night

   J So she will know how to grade the journals

21 What does the word <u>illustrate</u> mean in the section titled "Journal Information"?

   A To locate

   B To show

   C To name

   D To prove

22 Which sentence best describes how the article is organized?

   F It describes the events of Parents' Night.

   G It proves the importance of using journal.

   H It compares drawing with making a journal.

   J It tells the steps in order to make a journal.

© Houghton Mifflin Harcourt Publishing Company. All rights reserved.

Read this selection. Then answer the questions that follow it.
Mark your answer on the Answer Document.

Gathering Food

1 From the moment Adahy caught a glimpse of the big orange sun appearing over the mountain tops, he was positive that today would be a great day. Adahy and his friends would gather acorns to store for the winter months, an important task because the acorns would nourish the people in the cave when food was scarce.

2 Adahy anticipated his friends emerging from the cave, and then the three of them would start searching for acorns. As Adahy stared at the giant oak and hickory trees that surrounded the cave, he contemplated the various tasks assigned to each person who lived in the cave. The men constructed tools for hunting and fishing, while the women crafted pots and gathered berries, roots, and seeds to eat during winter.

3 Finally, Tooantuh and Sheasequat appeared. Sheasequat glanced at Adahy's empty hands and asked, "Adahy, do you have a pot to put the acorns in?"

4 "Oh, I forgot, but I will get it now," said Adahy. He disappeared into the cave and quickly returned with two large clay pots.

5 Adahy, Tooantuh, and Sheasequat started out on the path into the forest. The lofty trees towered over the boys, forming a tunnel into the woods. The boys were cautious about staying together and on the path. They listened closely to the sounds of the forest, straining their ears to hear squirrels chattering, a telltale sign of nearby acorns.

6 "Stop!" Tooantuh whispered, holding out his hand. "I think I hear them." The boys halted, looked up, and spotted several squirrels scampering among the trees.

7 "There they are," Sheasequat said. "Now we are sure to find what we need."

8   As squirrels scurried over their heads, Sheasequat, Tooantuh, and Adahy searched for acorns. They explored the forest around them and uncovered acorns under dried leaves and twigs. The squirrels found the acorns, too, in the oak branches above. Together the boys and the squirrels collected food for the winter; the squirrels would hoard them in their nests, while the people of the cave would store them in dirt holes to cool and preserve them.

9   When their pots were bursting with acorns, the boys returned to the path that would take them back to the cave. They would present the overflowing pots to Adsila, the food keeper, when they arrived.

10   "Adsila," they called proudly as they entered the cave. "Look what we have found."

11   Adsila turned to the boys and smiled. "You have done a great job. These acorns will feed many of us when it begins to snow. See what the women have collected for us." She gestured toward the holes in the cave floor.

12   Adahy and his friends peered into one of the holes in the dirt and saw seeds, roots, and nuts. The boys' pots of acorns made a significant contribution to the stores of winter food and would require a new hole. This winter, no one in the cave would go hungry.

13   Adahy was full of pride because he and his friends were helping to feed the cave families. He strolled out the cave entrance and gazed at the yellow sun setting behind the mountain tops against the rosy sky. Tomorrow would be an excellent day to forage for more food with Sheasequat and Tooantuh.

GO ON

© Houghton Mifflin Harcourt Publishing Company. All rights reserved.

23 Most of this story takes place—

A near a stream

B on a trail

C in a cave

D in a tree

24 What problem does Adahy face as he prepares for his task?

F He forgets his fishing tool.

G He forgets his clay pots.

H His friends disappear.

J His friends do not help him.

25 What is the best way to paraphrase the last sentence in paragraph 5?

A The squirrel's noises would lead them to acorns.

B The squirrel's noises would cause acorns to drop from the trees.

C The squirrels would have already collected the acorns.

D The squirrels would be so noisy that they would have to take another path.

26 Which word best describes Adahy and the other members of the cave families?

F Forgetful

G Lazy

H Over-confident

J Hard-working

27 Which sentence best describes the theme of the story?

A Caring for the environment makes the world a better place.

B Enjoying the simple things in life is important.

C Walking in nature results in happiness.

D Working together pays off in the end.

> ## Read this selection. Then answer the questions that follow it.
> ## Mark your answer on the Answer Document.

Fly High, Bessie Coleman

by Jane Sutcliffe

1   Two thousand people sat with their faces turned to the sky. High above the airfield, a pilot had just finished carving a crisp figure eight in the air. Suddenly, the plane seemed to stumble. Twisting and turning, it began to fall from the sky. The crowd watched in horror. Had something happened to the pilot?

2   But the woman in the cockpit of the plane on October 15, 1922, was in perfect control. Only two hundred feet above the ground she straightened out the tumbling aircraft and soared back into the sky. By the time she landed her plane, the crowd was on its feet, roaring with delight. Everyone cheered for Bessie Coleman, the first licensed black pilot in the world.

Coleman, in uniform, stands on the runner of a Model T Ford. The nose and right wing of her plane are to her left.

GO ON ➤

© Houghton Mifflin Harcourt Publishing Company. All rights reserved.

Growing Up

3   Bessie Coleman was born on January 26, 1892. She was a bright girl and a star pupil in school. In Waxahachie, Texas, where Bessie grew up, black children and white children attended different schools. Each year Bessie's school closed for months at a time. Instead of studying, the children joined their parents picking cotton on big plantations. Bessie's mother was proud of her daughter's sharp mind. She didn't want Bessie to spend her life picking cotton, and urged her to do something special with her life.

Learning to Fly

4   In 1915, when she was 23, Bessie Coleman moved to Chicago. She found a job as a manicurist in a men's barbershop. Coleman loved her job and the interesting people she met there. After the United States entered World War I in 1917, soldiers returning from the war often came to the shop. Coleman was fascinated by their stories of daredevil pilots. She read everything she could about airplanes and flying. She later recalled, "All the articles I read finally convinced me I should be up there flying and not just reading about it."

5   Bessie Coleman asked some of Chicago's pilots for lessons. They refused. No one thought that an African American woman could learn to fly.

6   In desperation, Coleman asked Robert Abbott for help. Abbott owned Chicago's African American newspaper, *The Chicago Defender*. He had often promised to help members of the black community with their problems. Abbott told Coleman to forget about learning to fly in the United States. Go to France, he said to her, where no one would care if her skin was black or white.

7   So she did. First Coleman learned to speak French. Then she applied to a French flying school and was accepted. On November 20, 1920, Coleman sailed for France, where she spent the next seven months taking flying lessons. She learned to fly straight and level, and to turn and bank the plane. She practiced making perfect landings. On a second trip to Europe, she spent months mastering rolls, loops, and spins. These were the tricks she would need if she planned to make her living as a performing pilot.

Performing in Airshows

8   Coleman returned to the United States in the summer of 1922. Wherever she performed, other African Americans wanted to know where they, too, could learn to fly. It was a question that made Coleman sad. She hoped that she could make enough money from her airshows to buy her own plane. Then she could open a school so everyone would have a chance to feel the freedom she felt in the sky.

9   By early 1923, Coleman was close to her goal. She had saved her money and bought a plane. Then, as she was flying to an airshow in California, her engine stalled. The brand-new plane crashed to the ground.

10   Coleman suffered a broken leg and three broken ribs. Still, she refused to quit. "Tell them all that as soon as I can walk I'm going to fly!" she wrote to friends and fans.

Coleman's pilot license was issued on June 15, 1921, in France. The year of her birth is incorrect. Bessie Coleman was born in 1892, not 1896.

GO ON

© Houghton Mifflin Harcourt Publishing Company. All rights reserved.

Name _____ Date _____

11   Many people, both black and white, were very impressed by Coleman's determination. A white businessman helped her buy another plane. By 1926, Coleman was back where she had been before the crash. She wrote to her sister, "I am right on the threshold of opening a school."

12   In 1929, three years after her death, the Bessie Coleman Aero Clubs were formed. The clubs encouraged and trained African American pilots—just as Coleman had hoped to do. In 1931, the clubs sponsored the first All-African-American airshow. Bessie Coleman would have been proud.

---

28 Which section of the article best explains how Bessie finds flying lessons?

F Growing Up

G Learning to Fly

H Performing in Air Shows

J The introduction

29 Which sentence from the article states an opinion?

A *Bessie Coleman would have been proud.*

B *She had saved her money and bought a plane.*

C *Then, as she was flying to an airshow in California, her engine stalled.*

D *Coleman suffered a broken leg and three broken ribs.*

30 Which of the following statements best describes why the author wrote this article?

F To persuade others to attend airshows

G To prove that France has the best pilot schools

H To describe a person who followed her dream and made it come true

J To explain that if you are different, it is difficult to get what you want

GO ON

31 Which sentence best describes how the article is organized?

A It tells the steps one must go through in order to become a famous pilot.

B It explains problems in learning to fly and how the problems are solved.

C It compares and contrasts flying with other daring performances.

D It explains the important events of one person's life in order.

32 If Bessie had lived longer, she most likely would have—

F gone back to France to learn more about flying

G taught other African Americans how to fly

H stopped writing letters to her sister

J gone back to being a manicurist

BE SURE TO MARK YOUR ANSWERS ON THE ANSWER DOCUMENT.

STOP

Name _____ Date _____

Writing: Revising and Editing

> **Read the introduction and the passage that follows it. Then read each question. Mark your answers on the Answer Document.**

Wendy wanted to learn about her favorite author. She did some research and wrote this report. Now she wants you to help her revise and edit the paper. Read Wendy's report and think about the changes she should make. Then answer the questions that follow.

Jeanne Birdsall

(1) Jeanne Birdsall is an award-winning children's author. (2) Birdsall says her sixth-grade teacher helped her develop creative thinking and writing skills.

(3) Her first book was *The Penderwicks: A Summer Tale of Four Sisters, Two Rabbits, and a Very Interesting Boy.* (4) Birdsall also wrote a sequel called *The Penderwicks On Gardam Street.* (5) In all, Birdsall plans to write a total of five books along the Penderwick family. (6) She says it takes her about three years to write one book.

(7) Birdsall bases her characters on real people and takes many ideas for her books from her life. (8) The Penderwicks are a really real family. (9) They are not perffect, and their problems could really happen to people. (10) Mr. Penderwick, the father, has four daughters.

GO ON

(11) Rosalind is the most oldest. (12) The other three daughters are Skye, Jane, and Batty. (13) The Penderwick children are a little bit like the children in Birdsall's family.

(14) Animals play a big part in Birdsall's life and they are important in her books, too. (15) Birdsall has many pets, including a dog named Cagney. (16) She named her dog after a gardener named Cagney in her Penderwick books. (17) While writing her first book, Birdsall had pet rabbits named Jane and Horatio. (18) She based a character's pets, Carla and Yaz, on her rabbits.

---

1 Which sentence could **BEST** be added after sentence 1?

A I read books by lots of other authors, too.

B She knew she wanted to be an author when she was only ten years old.

C The people who illustrate books can also win awards.

D I enjoy writing stories and hope to write a novel when I become an adult.

2 What change, if any, should be made in sentence 4?

F Change *wrote* to **wroet**

G Insert a comma after *called*

H Change *On* to **on**

J Make no change

Name _____ Date _____

3 What change should be made in sentence 5?

A Delete the comma after *all*

B Change *to* to **on**

C Change *books* to **book**

D Change *along* to **about**

4 What change should be made in sentence 8?

F Change *are* to **is**

G Change *a* to **an**

H Change *really real* to **realistic**

J Change the period to a comma

5 What change should be made in sentence 9?

A Change *perffect* to **perfect**

B Change *their* to **they're**

C Change *to* to **for**

D Change *people* to **peoples**

6 What change, if any, should be made in sentence 11?

F Change *is* to **be**

G Delete the word *most*

H Change *oldest* to **older**

J Make no change

7 What change should be made in sentence 14?

A Change *big* to **biggest**

B Change *Birdsall's* to **Birdsalls**

C Insert a comma after *life*

D Insert **also** after *and*

GO ON

Name _____ Date _____

Read the introduction and the passage that follows it. Then read each question. Mark your answers on the Answer Document.

Juan wrote this story about a memorable event. He wants you to review his paper. As you read, think about the corrections and improvements that Juan should make. Then answer the questions that follow.

A Balloon Ride

(1) Yesterday afternoon I went with my family to our town's annual hot-air balloon festival. (2) When we arrived, the balloons was not inflated. (3) Then, the pilots turned on the burners, and the balloons started to inflate. (4) Within minutes, the pilots lifted the balloons off the ground and transformed the sky into a polka-dot rainbow. (5) We watched from the ground as the balloons got smaller and smaller.

(6) At this point, we would usual leave the festival, but on this day my uncle took my hand and we strolled to a lone hot-air balloon. (7) I was stunned when the pilot opened the basket door and told us to step inside. (8) My mouth fell open, and I stared at the pilot in a days. (9) When my uncle explained that he had bought tickets for us to ride in the balloon, I couldn't believe my ears!

© Houghton Mifflin Harcourt Publishing Company. All rights reserved.

(10) Inside the basket, the pilot began by explaining the safety rules.

(11) He turned on the burner. (12) There was a loud whooshing sound as

a six-foot flame shot up into the balloon. (13) Eventually we lifted off the

pavemint and were soon soaring in the sky. (14) The pilot used the heated

air to control the movement of the balloon. (15) Neither my uncle or I could

believe how smooth the ride was.

(16) During the ride I asked the pilot a few questions, but I mainly just

enjoyed the peacefully ride. (17) Back on the ground, the pilot took our

picture to use in his advertisements. (18) What an exciting day!

---

8 What change should be made in sentence 2?

   F Change *we* to **we're**

   G Delete the comma after *arrived*

   H Change *was* to **were**

   J Change *inflated* to **inflate**

9 What change should be made in sentence 6?

   A Change *usual* to **usually**

   B Change *leave* to **leeve**

   C Delete the comma after *festival*

   D Change *uncle* to **Uncle**

GO ON

© Houghton Mifflin Harcourt Publishing Company. All rights reserved.

Name _____ Date _____

10 What change should be made in sentence 8?

  F Change *fell* to **fall**

  G Change *and* to **but**

  H Change *the pilot* to **he**

  J Change *days* to **daze**

11 Which transition word or phrase could **BEST** be added to the beginning of sentence 11?

  A In fact,

  B Next,

  C To summarize,

  D Last,

12 What change should be made in sentence 13?

  F Change *lifted* to **lift**

  G Change *off* to **of**

  H Change *pavemint* to **pavement**

  J Insert a comma after *soaring*

13 What change should be made in sentence 15?

  A Change *or* to **nor**

  B Change *I* to **me**

  C Change *believe* to **beleve**

  D Change *smooth* to **smoothly**

14 What change should be made in sentence 16?

  F Insert a comma after *During*

  G Change *asked* to **ask**

  H Insert a period after *questions*

  J Change *peacefully* to **peaceful**

GO ON

Read the introduction and the passage that follows it. Then read each question. Mark your answers on the Answer Document.

Marcel is in fourth grade. He wrote this report after he did research to learn about the Constitution. Marcel wants you to help him revise and edit the report. Read Marcel's report and think about the corrections and improvements he should make. Then answer the questions that follow.

The Constitution

(1) More than 200 years ago, a group of men came together to write the Constitution of the United States of america. (2) This document described how the United States government would work. (3) It may be the importantest document in the history of the United States. (4) It has governed the people of the United States since 1789.

(5) The authors of the Constitution knew that it might be necessary to change the document so they decided on the exact steps for how it could be changed. (6) In 1791, the first of these changes, called amendments, were added to the Constitution. (7) These first ten amendments. (8) Are called the Bill of Rights. (9) They protect the rights of the people of the United States. (10) The First Amendment gives people the freedom to follow any religion, or none at all. (11) It also protects freedom of speech, freedom of the press, and the right of people to gather together.

GO ON

(12) Over the years, other amendments have been added to the

Constitution. (13) In 1865, the Thirteenth Amendment ended slavery. (14) We

studied the end of slavery in school. (15) In 1920, the Nineteenth Amendment

gived women the right to vote. (16) Changes have also been made in recent

times. (17) In 1992, the Twenty-Seventh Amendment was added. (18) It states

that lawmakers cannot raise their pay while still in office.

(19) In the future, more changes will likely need to be made to the

Constitution. (20) Amendments will be suggested and lawmakers will vote

on them. (21) If most lawmakers agree with a change. (22) It will become

part of the Constitution.

15 What change should be made in sentence 1?

  A Delete the comma after *ago*

  B Change *group* to **groop**

  C Insert a period after *together*

  D Change *america* to **America**

16 What change should be made in sentence 3?

  F Change *be* to **been**

  G Change *importantest* to **most important**

  H Insert a comma after *document*

  J Change *history* to **historey**

GO ON

Name _____ Date _____

17 What change should be made in sentence 5?

   A Insert a comma after *Constitution*

   B Change *knew* to **know**

   C Insert a comma after *document*

   D Change *exact* to **exactly**

18 What revision, if any, is needed in sentences 7 and 8?

   F These first ten amendments are called the Bill of Rights.

   G These first ten amendments and are called the Bill of Rights.

   H These first ten amendments are called. The Bill of Rights.

   J No revision is needed.

19 What change should be made in sentence 15?

   A Delete the comma after *1920*

   B Change *gived* to **gave**

   C Change *women* to **womin**

   D Change *vote* to **voted**

20 What is the **BEST** way to rewrite sentences 21 and 22?

   F If most lawmakers agree with a change, it will become part of the Constitution.

   G If most lawmakers, agree with a change, so it will become part of the Constitution.

   H If most lawmakers agree. With a change, it will become part of the Constitution.

   J If most lawmakers agree, and a change will become part of the Constitution.

21 Which sentence does **NOT** belong in this paper?

   A Sentence 6

   B Sentence 11

   C Sentence 14

   D Sentence 18

© Houghton Mifflin Harcourt Publishing Company. All rights reserved.

Read the introduction and the passage that follows it. Then read each
question. Mark your answers on the Answer Document.

*Hannah wrote this story about a boy who enters a spelling bee. She would
like you to read her story and suggest the corrections and improvements she
should make. When you finish reading, answer the questions that follow.*

The Spelling Bee

(1) Robert always made very, really good grades on his spelling tests.

(2) His teacher, Mr. McNeil, challenged Robert to enter the school spelling

bee, and he accepted. (3) Robert thought winning the spelling bee would

be effortless.

(4) Mr. McNeil gave Robert a list of words to study to help him get

ready about the spelling bee. (5) When Robert scanned the list, he was

suddenly not so sure of hisself. (6) The words were so difficult he could

not even read some of them. (7) Many of the words had 16 letters, more

than half of all the letters in the alphabet. (8) Robert wondered if it was

too late to withdraw from the competition. (9) However, he did not want to

dissplease his teacher, so he decided to give it his best effort.

© Houghton Mifflin Harcourt Publishing Company. All rights reserved.

(10) Robert talked to his family about the spelling bee. (11) Everyone was excited about it, and said they would help him prepare. (12) His brother even promised to help him study every night. (13) For two weeks Robert practiced for at least one hour every day after school. (14) The words became easier to spell, and he made fewer guess.

(15) Robert won the school spelling bee and entered the city spelling bee. (16) What do you think happened? (17) The answer appeared on the front page of the community newspaper. (18) The article's headline read, "Local Boy wins Second Place." (19) Now Robert is studying for next year's competition!

---

22 What change, if any, should be made in sentence 1?

F Change *very, really good* to **excellent**

G Change *grades* to **grade**

H Change *on* to **to**

J Make no change

23 What change should be made in sentence 4?

A Change *Mr.* to **Mr**

B Change *gave* to **gived**

C Change *get* to **got**

D Change *about* to **for**

© Houghton Mifflin Harcourt Publishing Company. All rights reserved.

24 What change should be made in sentence 5?

  F Change *When* to **So**

  G Delete the comma after *list*

  H Change *suddenly* to **sudden**

  J Change *hisself* to **himself**

25 What change should be made in sentence 9?

  A Change *did not* to **did'nt**

  B Change *dissplease* to **displease**

  C Delete the comma after *teacher*

  D Change *effort* to **efort**

26 Which transition word or phrase could **BEST** be added to the beginning of sentence 10?

  F Tomorrow,

  G However,

  H That evening,

  J In conclusion,

27 What change, if any, should be made in sentence 14?

  A Change *became* to **become**

  B Change *easier* to **more easy**

  C Change *made* to **makes**

  D Change *guess* to **guesses**

28 What change, if any, should be made in sentence 18?

  F Change *article's* to **articles**

  G Change *read* to **is reading**

  H Change *wins* to **Wins**

  J Make no change

BE SURE TO MARK YOUR ANSWERS ON THE ANSWER DOCUMENT.

STOP

© Houghton Mifflin Harcourt Publishing Company. All rights reserved.

Writing: Written Composition

> Write a composition that explains how to prepare a simple breakfast.

Use a separate sheet of paper to plan your composition. Then write your composition on the lined pages that follow.

The information in the box below will help you remember what you should think about when you write your composition.

REMEMBER—YOU SHOULD

❏ write about how to prepare a simple breakfast

❏ begin with a topic sentence that introduces the process

❏ give step-by-step directions and use transition words such as *first, next,* and *last*

❏ conclude by describing the final results of the process

❏ try to use correct spelling, capitalization, punctuation, grammar, and sentences

Name _____ Date _____

© Houghton Mifflin Harcourt Publishing Company. All rights reserved.

Name _____ Date _____

_____

_____

_____

_____

_____

_____

_____

_____

_____

_____

_____

_____

_____

_____

© Houghton Mifflin Harcourt Publishing Company. All rights reserved.

Reading

> Read this selection. Then answer the questions that follow it.
> Mark your answers on the Answer Document.

At the Beach, At Last

Marina visited the beach last summer. Here is a story she wrote about one of her experiences.

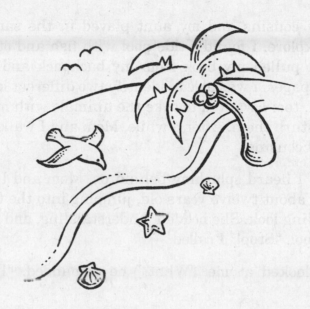

1   I've always wanted to visit the beach, and last summer I finally got to go. While there, I saw many people swimming, building <u>sandcastles</u>, and playing games. I did those things, too, but they are not what I enjoyed most. I got to <u>focus</u> on studying the wildlife that lives by the ocean, just like a marine biologist. A marine biologist is a scientist who studies living things that inhabit the ocean. I first learned about these scientists last year on a third-grade field trip to the city <u>aquarium</u>. Ever since then, I've wanted to be a marine biologist when I grow up.

2   Before our beach trip, I reread my favorite book, *Guide to the Seashore*, which I bought at the aquarium bookstore. At home, I packed the book, along with my clothes, hats, towels, water shoes, and sunscreen. For my <u>observations</u>, I packed a <u>spiral</u> notebook, pencils, a camera, and a magnifying glass. I couldn't wait to explore the beach like a <u>real</u> marine biologist.

© Houghton Mifflin Harcourt Publishing Company. All rights reserved.

3   Finally, it was time for our trip. My mother and I traveled by car with my aunt and my two cousins. After about six hours in the car, we arrived at the beach house we were renting for the week. Everyone was excited to get to the water, so we quickly put on our beach gear and sunscreen and walked down to the beach. I stood next to my mom and held her hand. The heavy air was unlike anything I had ever experienced. The wind carried the smell of salt water as it whipped my hair. I couldn't stop the smile that spread across my face. Finally, I was at the beach!

4   While my cousins and my aunt played in the sand, Mom and I started to explore. I found a tide pool with fish and other animals to <u>inspect</u>, so I pulled my book from my backpack and began flipping through the pages. I was able to identify two different kinds of fish and a sea urchin, too. I wanted to take the animals with me, but I knew I shouldn't disturb them. After a while, Mom and I walked back toward my aunt and cousins.

5   Suddenly, I heard splashing behind us. Mom and I turned around to see a boy, about twelve years old, jumping into the tide pool. I gave Mom a pleading look. She nodded, understanding, and we rushed back to the tide pool. "Stop!" I called.

6   The boy looked at me. "What?" he demanded. "I'm not hurting anything."

7   That's when I explained that he was, in fact, hurting something. He was disturbing the tide pool.

8   "The what?" he asked with a mixture of <u>anger</u> and confusion.

9   "You're jumping in a tide pool," I said. "The <u>shallow</u> water in a tide pool is actually home to many tiny living creatures. Just look."

10   The boy looked at his feet, shook his head, and mumbled, "<u>Impossible</u>." I encouraged him to look closer.

11   He bent down, placing his face near the water, and looked closely. "Wow!" he exclaimed. "There are things swimming in here."

12   "Yes, that's right," I said. "I have a book that explains all about the animals and their home. Do you want to learn about these tide pool creatures, too?"

GO ON

13 "Wow, you bet!" he agreed. Then Mom, the boy, and I sat down next to the tide pool and opened the book. I pointed out what I'd learned just moments before.

14 "Wow, you know a lot about marine animals."

15 "That's because I want to be a marine biologist," I said with <u>confidence</u>.

16 Another awe-inspired, "Wow," was all he could manage to say.

---

1 Most of this story takes place at a—

A beach

B school

C bookstore

D aquarium

2 In paragraph 1, the word <u>focus</u> means—

F create

G concentrate

H ignore

J remember

3 Use the dictionary entry below to answer the question.

> a•quar•i•um \ə-kwâr'-ē-əm\ *noun*
> **1.** a tank or bowl for living fish and plants **2.** a place for the public display of live animals and plants in water [from Latin *aquārium*, source of water]

What is the origin of the word <u>aquarium</u>?

A Latin

B Display

C Fish

D Public

GO ON

© Houghton Mifflin Harcourt Publishing Company. All rights reserved.

4 When the narrator arrives at the beach, she is eager to—

F smell the air

G explore the beach

H read her favorite book

J build a large sandcastle

5 Look at the word <u>real</u> in paragraph 2. Then complete this analogy: <u>Strong</u> is to <u>powerful</u> as <u>real</u> is to—

A clever

B adult

C curious

D genuine

6 The narrator first decided to become a marine biologist when she—

F spent a vacation at the beach

G bought a book about the beach

H identified the animals in a tide pool

J visited the city aquarium on a field trip

7 In paragraph 4, the word <u>inspect</u> means—

A move to the side

B not bother with

C look at carefully

D draw pictures of

8 The reader can tell that—

F tide pools are not important

G tide pools should be left alone

H nothing can live in a tide pool

J only fish can survive in a tide pool

9 How does the narrator feel when she sees the boy jumping in the tide pool?

A Upset

B Relieved

C Jealous

D Confused

10 The reader can tell that the narrator's mother—

F supports her daughter's interests

G is a scientist who studies the beach

H takes many vacations at the beach

J spends little time with her daughter

11 In paragraph 9, the word <u>shallow</u> means not—

A salty

B deep

C clear

D clean

GO ON

© Houghton Mifflin Harcourt Publishing Company. All rights reserved.
144

12 In paragraph 10, what does the word underline{impossible} mean?

F Not possible

G Very possible

H A little possible

J With possibility

13 Which words from the story show that the boy will stop jumping in tide pools?

A *"What?" he demanded. "I'm not hurting anything."*

B *"The what?" he asked with a mixture of anger and confusion.*

C *"Wow!" he exclaimed. "There are things swimming in here."*

D *"Wow, you know a lot about marine animals."*

14 What does the word underline{confidence} mean in paragraph 15?

F Ability to work

G Ability to learn

H Feeling of hope

J Feeling of certainty

15 Which consonant is silent in the word underline{sandcastles}?

A n

B c

C t

D l

16 Which of the following shows the correct way to stress the syllables in the word underline{observations}?

F OB • ser • va • tions

G ob • ser • va • TIONS

H ob • SER • va • tions

J ob • ser • VA • tions

17 Which of the following shows the correct way to divide the word underline{spiral} into syllables?

A sp • iral

B spi • ral

C spir • al

D spira • l

18 Which word has the same sound as the underlined part of the word underline{anger}?

F Frontier

G Declare

H Professor

J Before

GO ON

Read this selection. Then answer the questions that follow it.
Mark your answers on the Answer Document.

How to Save Water

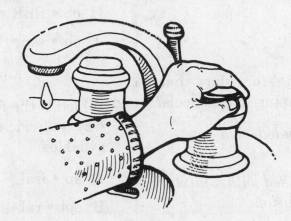

1   Have you ever been around when the water bill arrives at your house? Perhaps you've heard someone say, "Stop wasting water! The water bill is sky high!" Water costs a lot of <u>money</u>. Reducing the amount of water you use not only helps lower your family's water bill, but also helps the environment.

2   You might be wondering why water is so expensive. After all, water hardly seems <u>scarce</u>. It covers the majority of Earth, right? While that is true, most of Earth's water is in salty oceans. Because we cannot drink salt water, only a small amount of Earth's water is drinkable.

3   All living things need water to survive, so water is one of our most important natural resources. With a little <u>effort</u>, you can conserve water and also help keep down the water bill. You will be surprised at how easy it is to save water. Read the tips below to learn how.

Inside

4   From the time you wake up until you go to bed, pay attention to how much water you use. How can you save water?

5   Do you wash your hands before you eat breakfast? If you do, turn off the water while you lather the soap. Then, when you finish washing your

hands, make sure you turn the faucet all the way off. Also remember to turn off the faucet when you put toothpaste on your toothbrush and while brushing your teeth. If your faucet drips when it is off, see if it can be fixed. If you have some trash to <u>dispose</u> of, do not put it in the toilet. Use a trashcan instead.

6   Maybe you take a <u>shower</u> in the morning. Try to keep your time in the shower to less than ten minutes. Installing a low-flow showerhead, which reduces the amount of water you use, will help, too. Here is an interesting fact: If everyone in the United States shortened their showers by just a couple of minutes, it would conserve more than 80 billion gallons of water each year! If you let the water in the shower heat up before you get in, don't let it go down the drain. You can catch the water in buckets and use it to water houseplants or your lawn.

7   Usually you use much less water in a shower than in a bath. A shower is more refreshing, too. However, if you decide to take a bath, be sure to close the drain before you turn on the water. There's no need to let the water warm up first. Remember to adjust the water temperature so that it is not too hot.

Outside

8   Be an inspector and check all outdoor faucets for leaks. If you find a leaky faucet, fix it with a <u>wrench</u>. For the lawn, use grasses and other plants that need a minimal amount of water. When you water your lawn, make sure to do it either early in the morning or late in the evening. Watering during the hottest hours of the day <u>increases</u> evaporation. For example, if you water your lawn at 2:00 P.M., more than half of the water can evaporate. Watch where you are watering, too, and adjust any <u>sprinklers</u> that are watering your driveway or a sidewalk.

9   There are so many ways to save water. For fun, try to do at least one thing every day to conserve water. Do your <u>community</u> a <u>favor</u> and tell your friends some tips for conserving water, too. They will probably thank you. Every drop of water counts!

GO ON

© Houghton Mifflin Harcourt Publishing Company. All rights reserved.

19 What does the word <u>scarce</u> mean in paragraph 2?

  A Invisible

  B Costly

  C Usable

  D Limited

20 The reader can conclude that—

  F people who take baths do not care about the environment

  G lawns and gardens should never be watered when the sky is dark

  H if people could drink salt water, there would be less need to save water

  J the biggest waste of water comes from washing hands and brushing teeth

21 In paragraph 3, the word <u>effort</u> means—

  A work

  B cause

  C patience

  D imagination

22 Which sentence from the selection is an opinion?

  F *While that is true, most of Earth's water is in salty oceans.*

  G *You will be surprised at how easy it is to save water.*

  H *You can catch the water in buckets and use it to water houseplants or your lawn.*

  J *Usually you use much less water in a shower than in a bath.*

23 What does the word <u>dispose</u> mean in paragraph 5?

  A Waste

  B Look for

  C Clean up

  D Get rid of

24 The article pointed out that people can save water in the shower by—

  F using a low-flow showerhead

  G adjusting the water temperature

  H turning the water off while lathering the soap

  J closing the drain before turning on the water

GO ON ➡

© Houghton Mifflin Harcourt Publishing Company. All rights reserved.

25 In paragraph 7, the author says "A shower is more refreshing, too." What makes this statement an opinion?

A The author wrote it.

B It is the author's belief.

C Most people agree with it.

D It can be proven true or false.

26 Look at the word <u>increases</u> in paragraph 8. Then complete this analogy: <u>Repairs</u> is to <u>breaks</u> as <u>increases</u> is to—

F wastes

G grows

H lowers

J appears

27 What is paragraph 8 mainly about?

A The types of grasses and plants to use in a lawn

B The hottest part of the day

C Where to check for leaky faucets

D How to use less water in the yard

28 In paragraph 8, the word <u>sprinklers</u> means things that—

F leak water

G spray water

H save water

J evaporate water

29 In paragraph 9, what does the word <u>community</u> mean?

A The opposite of your friends

B A single person, not in a group

C A group of people living together

D The water source closest to your house

30 In paragraph 9, what does the word <u>favor</u> mean?

F A list of tips

G A secret to tell

H An act of kindness

J A command to follow

GO ON

© Houghton Mifflin Harcourt Publishing Company. All rights reserved.

Name _____ Date _____

31 Look at the chart below and use it to answer the question below.

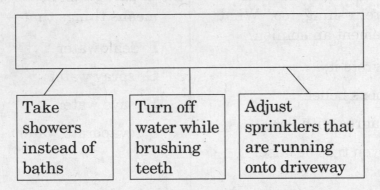

| Take showers instead of baths | Turn off water while brushing teeth | Adjust sprinklers that are running onto driveway |

Which of the following belongs in the empty box?

A Where water comes from

B Ways to save water at home

C Why water costs a lot of money

D How people waste water in the bathroom

---

32 What generalization can the reader make from this selection?

F Leaky faucets can waste a lot of water.

G There is much people can do to save water at home.

H Most people do not care about saving water.

J People usually leave the water on while brushing teeth.

33 Which word has the same sound as the underlined part of the word m<u>o</u>ney?

A Phone

B Dune

C Stoop

D Crumb

34 Which of these shows the correct way to divide the word <u>shower</u> into syllables?

F sh • ower

G show • er

H showe • r

J sho • wer

35 Which letter is silent in the word <u>wrench</u>?

A w

B r

C e

D n

BE SURE TO MARK YOUR ANSWERS ON THE ANSWER DOCUMENT. STOP

© Houghton Mifflin Harcourt Publishing Company. All rights reserved.

Writing: Revising and Editing

Evan is in fourth grade. He wrote this paper to tell about his teacher. He wants you to read the paper and help him improve it. As you read, think about the suggestions you would give Evan. Then answer the questions that follow.

Mr. Ward's Lessons

(1) Mine teacher, Mr. Ward, has always been interested in science and the Arctic. (2) Last year, he traveled to the northern part of Alaska to study one of the chilliest places on Earth. (3) This year, wev'e learned about the Arctic from his stories and pictures. (4) In third grade, my teacher was Mrs. Vargas.

(5) Mr. Ward has shown us pictures of some of the animals he saw while in Alaska. (6) My favorite pictures were of polear bears. (7) These huge bears have features that help them survive in the extreme cold. (8) They have thicker fur than other bears. (9) Their feet work like oars to help them swim gracefuller, too. (10) A thick layer of blubber helps keep them warm and float in the icy water.

(11) We also learned about the walrus. (12) Mr. Ward told us that a bear might try to hunt a walrus. (13) A walrus can defend it with its long tusks. (14) A walrus also uses its tusks to climb onto the ice from the water. (15) A walrus is a huge animal. (16) An adult male walrus, called a bull, may weigh as much as one ton.

(17) Because of Mr. Ward's teaching, I hope to travel to one of the very colder places on Earth to study the animals that live there. (18) Then I can share my knowledge with others, too, just like Mr. Ward.

GO ON

© Houghton Mifflin Harcourt Publishing Company. All rights reserved.

1 What change should be made in sentence 1?

   A Change *Mine* to **My**

   B Delete the comma after **Ward**

   C Change *has* to **have**

   D Change *interested* to **interests**

2 What change, if any, should be made in sentence 3?

   F Change *This* to **These**

   G Change *wev'e* to **we've**

   H Change *stories* to **story's**

   J Make no change

3 What change, if any, should be made in sentence 6?

   A Change *My* to **Me**

   B Change *favorite* to **most favoritest**

   C Change *polear* to **polar**

   D Make no change

4 What change should be made in sentence 9?

   F Change *Their* to **There**

   G Change *feet* to **foots**

   H Change *swim* to **swam**

   J Change *gracefuller* to **more gracefully**

5 What change, if any, should be made in sentence 13?

   A Change *defend* to **defends**

   B Change *it* to **itself**

   C Change *its* to **it's**

   D Make no change

6 What change should be made in sentence 17?

   F Change *Ward's* to **Wards**

   G Delete the comma after **teaching**

   H Change *colder* to **coldest**

   J Change *live* to **lives**

7 Which sentence does **NOT** belong in this paper?

   A Sentence 4

   B Sentence 8

   C Sentence 14

   D Sentence 18

GO ON

© Houghton Mifflin Harcourt Publishing Company. All rights reserved.

> **Read the introduction and the passage that follows it. Then read each question. Mark your answers on the Answer Document.**

Katherine wrote this story about something that happened to her. She wants you to read her paper and think about the corrections she should make to improve it. When you finish reading, answer the questions that follow.

No Fun

(1) My next-door neighbor, Alexa, broke her arm a few months ago.

(2) She got a cast, and I really liked it's bright orange color. (3) Everyone in class liked the cast, too, and they signed the cast to wish Alexa well.

(4) The cast was on her left arm and shes left-handed, so she was unable to write. (5) Since I sat next to her, I volunteered to write for her in class.

(6) From watching Alexa, it looked like having a broken arm had a lot of benefits. (7) I didn't realize it at the time, but I would soon learn how wrong my assumption was.

(8) Last week, I was riding my bike more faster than normal, and I fell. (9) I was wearing my helmet, of course, so I did not injure my head, but I did hurt my right wrist. (10) The doctor lined up the bones correctly and put a cast over my arm. (11) She said that while I wear the cast for six weeks, new bone cells will grow, and my bone will be as good as new.

(12) The next day at school, I asked everyone to sign my cast. (13) I

tried to sign it my self, but it was much harder than I thought. (14) By

lunch, my arm was itchy, and I couldn't scratch it. (15) It felt hot and

sweaty, too. (16) So far, wearing the cast is no fun. (17) I'll definitely be the

most slowest bike rider on my block once the cast is off, and I'll be careful

about what I wish for!

---

8 What change should be made in sentence 2?

   F Change *got* to **gets**

   G Change *I* to **me**

   H Change *it's* to **its**

   J Change *orange* to **oranje**

9 What is the **BEST** way to rewrite sentence 3?

   A In class everyone in it liked the cast and they signed the cast to wish Alexa well, too.

   B Everyone in class liked the cast, too, and they signed it to wish Alexa well.

   C Everyone in class liked, signed, and wished the cast to wish Alexa well.

   D It was liked, too, by everyone in class, and they signed it to wish Alexa well.

10 What change should be made in sentence 4?

   F Change *shes* to **she's**

   G Insert a period after *left-handed*

   H Change *unable* to **unabel**

   J Change *to* to **for**

11 What change should be made in sentence 8?

   A Delete the comma after *Yesterday*

   B Change *was* to **were**

   C Delete the word *more*

   D Change *fell* to **fallen**

GO ON

12 Which sentence could **BEST** be added after sentence 9?

F My favorite color is green, so I got a green cast on my arm.

G Unlike Alex, I am right-handed, so I write with my right hand.

H I always wear a helmet when I go skating, too.

J At the hospital, an X-ray showed that the bone just above my wrist was broken.

13 What change should be made in sentence 13?

A Change *my self* to **myself**

B Change *but* to **until**

C Change *much harder* to **much more harder**

D Change *thought* to **thinking**

14 What change should be made in sentence 17?

F Change *definitely* to **definite**

G Delete *most* before *slowest*

H Change *once* to **one**

J Change *careful* to **carefull**

GO ON

> **Read each introduction and the passage that follows it. Then read each question. Mark your answers on the Answer Document.**

Malik wrote this story about a family that enjoys a challenge. He wants you to help him with the revising and editing before he turns the story in to his teacher. Read the story and think about the changes he should make. Then answer the questions that follow.

A Simple Answer

(1) Everyone in my family enjoys a challenging riddle. (2) In the mornings, we take turns writing a riddle for everyone else to solve.

(3) The one I wrote this morning took more long than usual to unravel.

(4) Here is what I wrote: What is the beginning of every end and the end of time and space?

(5) I watched my family as they carefully read the sentence. (6) There brows furrowed as they reread the question. (7) My father, usually the most creative, scratched his head. (8) My mother repeated the question over and over. (9) My brother and sister gave many answers, but they were all incorrect. (10) Finally, it was time to leave for work and school, and no one had identified the correct answer.

(11) That evening, my brother declared that hed given up trying to solve the puzzle, and my sister was convinced there was no correct solution.

GO ON

(12) I offered to tell them, but they said they wanted to solve it theirself.

(13) However, they asked for a hint, so I suggested that everyone read it one last time and look at the words more closer. (14) My entire family thought very very very hard and made a final effort to solve the puzzle.

(15) Then a huge smile slowly grew across my sister's face and she exclaimed, "I've got it! (16) The answer is the letter e! It's the beginning of the words *every* and *end*. (17) It's also at the end of the words *time* and *space*!"

(18) My nodding head and knowing smirk told her that she had indeed found the solution. (19) My sister was so proud of her.

---

15 What change should be made in sentence 3?

  A Change *The* to **That**

  B Change *wrote* to **written**

  C Change *more long* to **longer**

  D Change *usual* to **usually**

16 What change, if any, should be made in sentence 6?

  F Change *There* to **Their**

  G Change *as* to **during**

  H Change the period to a question mark

  J Make no change

17 What change should be made in sentence 11?

  A Delete the comma after *evening*

  B Change *hed* to **he'd**

  C Delete the comma after *puzzle*

  D Change *correct* to **correctly**

18 What change should be made in sentence 12?

  F Change *offered* to **offer**

  G Change *but* to **since**

  H Change *solve* to **solving**

  J Change *theirself* to **themselves**

GO ON

19 What change should be made in sentence 13?

    A Delete the comma after *However*

    B Change *so* to **as a result**

    C Insert a comma after *one*

    D Change *closer* to **closely**

20 What change should be made in sentence 14?

    F Change *family* to **families**

    G Change *very very very hard* to **even harder**

    H Change *final* to **lastly**

    J Change *solve* to **solved**

21 What change should be made in sentence 19?

    A Change *My* to **Mine**

    B Change *sister* to **Sister**

    C Change *proud* to **prouder**

    D Change *her* to **herself**

GO ON

© Houghton Mifflin Harcourt Publishing Company. All rights reserved.

Read the introduction and the passage that follows it. Then read each question. Mark your answers on the Answer Document.

So Yee wrote this report about a game she thought was interesting. She want you to read her report and think about the changes she should make to improve it. When you finish reading, answer the questions that follow.

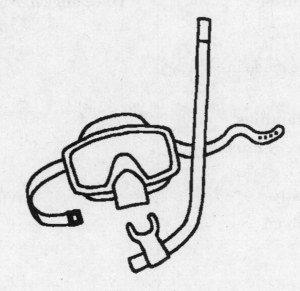

Underwater Hockey

(1) Do you like to swim? (2) Do you also like hockey? (3) If you said

"yes" to these two questions, perhaps you're like the game "octopush."

(4) It's also known as underwater hockey. (5) A group of scuba divers in

Britain invented the game in 1954. (6) Today the sport is becoming more

popular. (7) It is offen played in places around the world.

© Houghton Mifflin Harcourt Publishing Company. All rights reserved.

(8) An underwater hockey game is played with two teams. (9) Each team has six players. (10) The game takes place at the bottom of a swimming pool. (11) Players wear flippers, a diving mask, a glove, a snorkel, and a cap to protect they're ears. (12) They use speciel sticks about as long as a ruler to hit and slide a heavy puck along the bottom of the pool. (13) There is a goal at each end of the pool. (14) One team as in regular hockey tries to get the puck into the other team's goal and this is how you score.

(15) It is important for teammates to work together if they want to score many points. (16) Players "talk" to and answer each other by tapping their sticks on the bottom of the pool. (17) A person's size does not matter. (18) Because you're practically weightless in the water, everyone is equal. (19) It doesn't matter if you are the bigger person or the smallest person. (20) If you enjoy swimming underwater, this is a game you will really like a lot.

GO ON

© Houghton Mifflin Harcourt Publishing Company. All rights reserved.

22 What change, if any, should be made in sentence 3?

   F Change *said* to **saying**

   G Change *these* to **this**

   H Change *you're* to **you'd**

   J Make no change

23 What change, if any, should be made in sentence 7?

   A Change *It is* to **Its**

   B Change *offen* to **often**

   C Change *world* to **World**

   D Make no change

24 What change should be made in sentence 11?

   F Change *Players* to **Player**

   G Change *wear* to **wore**

   H Insert a comma after *cap*

   J Change *they're* to **their**

25 What change should be made in sentence 12?

   A Change *speciel* to **special**

   B Change *about* to **around**

   C Change *long* to **longer**

   D Change *of* to **on**

26 What is the **BEST** way to rewrite sentence 14?

   F As in regular hockey, one team tries to score a goal by getting the puck into the other team's goal.

   G One team in underwater hockey tries to get the puck, as in regular hockey, into the other team's goal to score a goal.

   H As in regular hockey and in underwater hockey, one team tries to score a goal by getting the puck into the other team's goal.

   J In regular hockey, one team tries to get the puck into the other team's goal to score and it is as this how you score in underwater hockey.

27 What change should be made in sentence 19?

   A Change *doesn't* to **don't**

   B Change *bigger* to **biggest**

   C Change *or* to **and**

   D Change *smallest* to **more smaller**

28 What change should be made in sentence 20?

   F Change *If* to **So**

   G Change *enjoy* to **enjoying**

   H Change *swimming* to **swimmer**

   J Change *really like a lot* to **love**

BE SURE TO MARK YOUR ANSWERS ON THE ANSWER DOCUMENT.

STOP

© Houghton Mifflin Harcourt Publishing Company. All rights reserved.

Writing: Written Composition

> Write about a beautiful or interesting thing you have seen in nature. Choose two of the following genres that will best help you tell about your topic: poetry, journal entry, expository nonfiction, fiction, advertisement, or friendly letter.

Use a separate sheet of paper to plan your composition. Then write your composition on the lined pages that follow.

The information in the box below will help you remember what you should think about when you write your composition.

> REMEMBER—YOU SHOULD
>
> ❑ choose two different genres that will best help you write about a beautiful or interesting thing you have seen in nature
>
> ❑ for each genre you choose, include details that suit that genre
>
> ❑ present different ideas about the topic in each genre
>
> ❑ use exact details to support your main ideas
>
> ❑ try to use correct spelling, capitalization, punctuation, grammar, and sentences

_____

_____

_____

_____

_____

_____

_____

_____

_____

_____

_____

_____

_____

_____

© Houghton Mifflin Harcourt Publishing Company. All rights reserved.

_____

_____

_____

_____

_____

_____

_____

_____

_____

_____

_____

_____

_____

_____

_____

_____

Name _____ Date _____

Justin and the Best Biscuits in the World

> **Think back to the novel *Justin and the Best Biscuits in the World* to answer questions 1–10. Fill in the correct answers on the Answer Document.**

1 In Chapter 1, the story begins at—

   A a store

   B a playground

   C Justin's house

   D Anthony's house

2 Hadiya is best described as—

   F careless

   G fearful

   H neat

   J silly

3 How can the reader tell that Anthony is a kind person?

   A He sits on Justin's lumpy bed.

   B He helps Justin clean his room.

   C He tells Justin about his grandmother.

   D He plays basketball with Justin and Evelyn.

4 Which word best describes Grandpa?

   F Brave

   G Crabby

   H Patient

   J Rude

5 How does the author show that Justin and Grandpa have a special bond?

   A Justin and Grandpa laugh about the messy room.

   B Grandpa goes into Justin's room when he comes to visit.

   C Grandpa tells Justin about African American cowhands and the rodeo.

   D Justin sits on his bed and looks at Grandpa without moving.

GO ON

© Houghton Mifflin Harcourt Publishing Company. All rights reserved.

6 Which of the following sentences helps the reader visualize how Justin looked when he went to Grandpa's ranch?

F *Later that evening Justin packed his duffel bag.*

G *He was so excited about going with Grandpa he couldn't sleep.*

H *He polished his cowboy boots and shined his silver cowboy belt buckle.*

J *Justin lay in his bed imagining himself riding upon a horse under a dark starlit sky.*

7 Which of the following sentences states an opinion?

A Grandpa's ranch is quiet and tranquil.

B Railroads link the country from East to West.

C Black Lightning is the youngest of three horses.

D Justin's great-great-grandfather rides cattle trails from Texas to Kansas.

8 In Chapter 5, Justin learns how to—

F make a bed

G catch fireflies

H cook biscuits and beans

J ride a horse without a saddle

9 In Chapter 7, what lesson does Grandpa teach Justin?

A Housework is for women.

B The better you do a job the easier it becomes.

C Bill Picket was the greatest cowhand that ever lived.

D Only men can learn how to take care of horses and cattle.

10 Justin most likely wants to bake biscuits for his family to—

F make Evelyn mad at him

G share a treat with his best friend Anthony

H show that he was a better cook than Hadiya

J show how much he had changed while visiting Grandpa

BE SURE TO MARK YOUR ANSWERS ON THE ANSWER DOCUMENT.

© Houghton Mifflin Harcourt Publishing Company. All rights reserved.

Name _____ Date _____

Phineas L. MacGuire... Gets Slimed!

> Think back to the novel *Phineas L. MacGuire...Gets Slimed!* to answer questions 1–10. Fill in the correct answers on the Answer Document.

1 Mac's goal at the beginning of the story is to—

A make a volcano

B be called Listerman

C teach Sparky how to talk

D be the best fourth-grade scientist

2 How does the reader know that Mac does not live close to his school?

F He changes his goals.

G He dreams of being a superhero.

H He rides the bus to get to his house.

J He is dragging his backpack down the street.

3 Which word best describes Mac in Chapter 2?

A Gloomy

B Messy

C Stern

D Uneasy

4 Sarah cleans the refrigerator because—

F Mac made a mess in it

G Margaret spilled juice in it

H Mac's mom offered to pay her extra

J she was looking for something to feed Margaret

5 Which event happens first in Chapter 4?

A Mac changes his goals.

B Ben raises his hand to run for class president.

C Mac and Aretha talk on the jungle gym at recess.

D Mrs. Tuttle blows the whistle to tell the students to come inside.

GO ON

Name _____   Date _____

6 In Chapter 5, which of the following events shows that Mac has both good and bad things happen in his life?

F His best friend moves away, but Aretha becomes his new best friend.

G He gets the teacher he wants, but he gets the babysitter he does not want.

H He has to write a book report, but he is able to write it about a book he has already read.

J His mom and stepdad are going away for the weekend, but his dad is going to take care of him.

7 What happens when Ben asks Mac to be his vice president?

A Mac laughs at Ben.

B Mac turns Ben down.

C Mac thinks it is a great idea.

D Mac draws a poster for their campaign.

8 What does Ben do to get Aretha to be his vice president?

F He starts to tell jokes.

G He pays her some money.

H He tells her a bunch of lies.

J He promises to do her chores.

9 Which conclusion can the reader draw about Mac based on information in Chapter 13?

A Mac has moved several times.

B Mac thinks Ben is the smartest kid he knows.

C Mac keeps his desk clean so he can do experiments.

D Mac always checks in with Sarah as soon as he gets home.

10 Ben's dad flies in from Seattle because—

F Ben is elected president

G Ben is elected vice president

H Ben builds a mold museum for Mac

J Ben wins first place in the science fair

BE SURE TO MARK YOUR ANSWERS ON THE ANSWER DOCUMENT.

STOP

© Houghton Mifflin Harcourt Publishing Company. All rights reserved.

Name _____ Date _____

Sea Turtles: Ocean Nomads

> **Think back to the novel *Sea Turtles: Ocean Nomads* to answer questions 1–10.
> Fill in the correct answers on the Answer Document.**

1 What setting is described at the beginning of this book?

A A desert

B A grassy plain

C A tropical island

D A snow-capped mountain

2 What is the topic of this book?

F Parrot fish

G Sea turtles

H Rain forests

J Coral caves

3. Parrot fish have teeth that are fused together so they can—

A eat shellfish

B hold on to sea plants

C grind up chunks of coral

D crush the bones of sea turtles

4. How are humans and sea turtles alike?

F They breathe air.

G They have a hard shell.

H They usually live on land.

J They are types of reptiles.

5 Tar is a problem for sea turtles because it—

A makes it difficult for them to breathe

B makes it harder for them to stay afloat

C covers their eyes, nose, and mouth

D softens their shell, flippers, and beak

6 Which of the following animals is most like a sea turtle?

F Fish

G Bird

H Horse

J Snake

GO ON

© Houghton Mifflin Harcourt Publishing Company. All rights reserved.

Name _____ Date _____

7 Scientists want to learn from their experiment with Myrtle how—

A turtles eat

B turtles see

C turtles hear

D turtles breathe

8 Which of the following is a source of noise pollution that could affect sea turtles?

F Ship engines

G Whales singing

H People's voices

J Waves crashing

9 The first few days of a sea turtle's life are the most dangerous because it has to—

A look for its mother in the sea

B find food as soon as it hatches

C cross the beach to get to the ocean

D dig out of the sand without being able to see

10 Which conclusion can the reader draw from this book?

F Water pollution never affects sea turtles.

G Soon there will not be any sea turtles left.

H Many people are trying to help sea turtles.

J Sea turtles should only live in marine parks.

BE SURE TO MARK YOUR ANSWERS ON THE ANSWER DOCUMENT.

© Houghton Mifflin Harcourt Publishing Company. All rights reserved.